• • •
• • •
• • •

Praise for *What If?*

The ability to identify problems worth solving and deal with uncertainty with creativity is required of everyone living in a rapidly changing world. In *What If?*, Beghetto beautifully presents a brilliant conceptual framework and ultra-practical strategies and tools to cultivate this ability in classrooms. A must-read for all teachers who want to transform their teaching.

—Yong Zhao, Foundation Distinguished Professor, University of Kansas, author of Reach for Greatness: Personalizable Education for All Children

Ron Beghetto's book encourages educators to move beyond rote tasks and take on complex and creative challenges within schools. With exemplars for how to support this work in classrooms, this book will help educators reimagine instruction and help us all believe in the power of generative thinking.

—Laura McBain, K12 Lab Director of Community and Implementation, d. school, Stanford University

Cultivating complex problem-solving skills in all students is one of the most important challenges for all of us involved in education today. This scholarly and practical book is the perfect companion for any teacher looking to understand the full spectrum of challenges from the relatively straightforward in the classroom to the wilder and less certain ones lurking in the real world.

—Bill Lucas, Professor of Learning, University of Winchester, UK, Co-Chair PISA 2021 Creative Thinking Test, author of Teaching Creative Thinking

With wit and insight, Ron Beghetto offers strategies for blending the rigid and mundane world of the traditional classroom with the untethered uncertainty of real-world problems.

—Gregory Reeves, Gifted and Talented Specialist, Region 17 Education Service Center, Lubbock, TX

RONALD A. BEGHETTO

WHAT IF?

BUILDING STUDENTS' PROBLEM-SOLVING SKILLS THROUGH COMPLEX CHALLENGES

ASCD®

Alexandria, Virginia USA

1703 N. Beauregard St. • Alexandria, VA 22311-1714 USA
Phone: 800-933-2723 or 703-578-9600 • Fax: 703-575-5400
Website: www.ascd.org • E-mail: member@ascd.org
Author guidelines: www.ascd.org/write

Deborah S. Delisle, *Executive Director*; Stefani Roth, *Publisher*; Genny Ostertag, *Director, Content Acquisitions*; Susan Hills, *Acquisitions Editor*; Julie Houtz, *Director, Book Editing & Production*; Miriam Calderone, *Editor*; Judi Connelly, *Associate Art Director*; Georgia Park, *Senior Graphic Designer*; Circle Graphics, *Typesetter*; Mike Kalyan, *Director, Production Services*; Shajuan Martin, *E-Publishing Specialist*; Sue Curran, *Production Specialist*

All web links in this book are correct as of the publication date below but may have become inactive or otherwise modified since that time. If you notice a deactivated or changed link, please e-mail books@ascd.org with the words "Link Update" in the subject line. In your message, please specify the web link, the book title, and the page number on which the link appears.

PAPERBACK ISBN: 978-1-4166-2641-1   ASCD product #118009
PDF E-BOOK ISBN: 978-1-4166-2642-8; see Books in Print for other formats.
ASCD Member Book No. FY19-4B (Jan. 2019 PS). Member books mail to Premium (P), Select (S), and Institutional Plus (I+) members on this schedule: Jan, PSI+; Feb, P; Apr, PSI+; May, P; Jul, PSI+; Aug, P; Sep, PSI+; Nov, PSI+; Dec, P. For details, see www.ascd.org/membership and www.ascd.org/memberbooks.

Quantity discounts are available: e-mail programteam@ascd.org or call 800-933-2723, ext. 5773, or 703-575-5773. For desk copies, go to www.ascd.org/deskcopy.

Library of Congress Cataloging-in-Publication Data

Names: Beghetto, Ronald A., 1969- author.
Title: What if? : building students' problem-solving skills through complex challenges / Ronald A. Beghetto.
Description: Alexandria, VA : ASCD, 2018. | Includes bibliographical references and index.
Identifiers: LCCN 2018017958 (print) | LCCN 2018019903 (ebook) | ISBN 9781416626428 (PDF) | ISBN 9781416626411 (pbk.)
Subjects: LCSH: Critical thinking—Study and teaching. | Problem solving—Study and teaching.
Classification: LCC LB1590.3 (ebook) | LCC LB1590.3 .B43 2018 (print) | DDC 370.15/2—dc23
LC record available at https://lccn.loc.gov/2018017958

27 26 25 24 23 22 21 20 19 18   1 2 3 4 5 6 7 8 9 10 11 12

· · ·
· · ·
· · ·

For my daughter Olivia:
May you always have the courage
to give voice to your beautiful ideas,
so they can grow in the world and make
a lasting and positive contribution to others.

· · ·
· · ·
· · ·

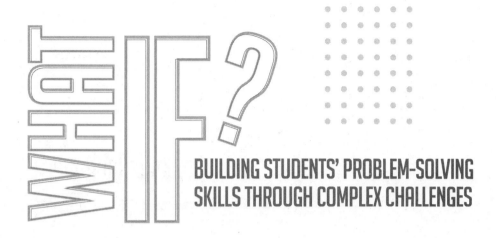

WHAT IF?

BUILDING STUDENTS' PROBLEM-SOLVING SKILLS THROUGH COMPLEX CHALLENGES

Acknowledgments

I would like to thank all the students, teachers, and colleagues whom I have had the privilege of working with over the past two decades. I am also grateful to Susan Hills, my incredibly helpful and encouraging acquisitions editor at ASCD, Miriam Calderone for her thorough and thoughtful editing, and everyone at ASCD for their assistance along the way! Finally, I would like to thank all my family and friends, especially my wife Jeralynn and daughter Olivia, who provide inspiration and persistent support.

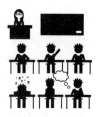

Introduction

Toward the end of 3rd grade, my daughter got in trouble for passing a note in class. The note read, "I hate this worksheet factory!" I found this somewhat humorous and even beautiful in its resistance, but also a bit disconcerting. When we talked about it, my daughter explained that she didn't like how she was asked to learn in school. She preferred challenging herself to craft accessories for her dolls and gifts for friends and family, seeking out and putting her own twist on information she gleaned from YouTube videos and other resources.

I explained to her that the worksheets in school were practice exercises that could help her learn important information and skills and that even if she didn't see the value in what she was practicing now, she might someday realize its benefit. Perhaps unsurprisingly, my daughter did not find my argument compelling or persuasive.

I admit that weakly appealing to the Neverland of "someday" has never sat well with me as a parent or as an educator—but neither has the idea that learning should somehow always be easy, fun, or immediately applicable. Deep domain knowledge is necessary for competence in any field, and developing that knowledge takes guided practice, persistence, and a lot of hard work (Ericsson, Krampe, & Tesch-Römer, 1993). Like many important endeavors in life, the process isn't always fun. Moreover, not everything we learn or know needs to have immediate or even future *practical* value. There is beauty to be found from delving deeply into a subject area; the process can be challenging and rewarding in itself.

Still, my daughter had a point. Schools are not giving students enough opportunities to grapple with complex challenges. Instead, we go to great lengths to clearly define the problems that students will solve, how they should solve them, and what the outcomes should be. Such assignments have their place—students do learn from working through routine assignments that have predetermined outcomes and ways of obtaining those outcomes (Lee & Anderson, 2013), and learning thrives in a supportive and structured environment (Reeve, 2009)—but relying too much on this type of learning experience has serious drawbacks.

The Power of the Unknown

Given that a fundamental goal of school is to prepare young people for the unknowable future, it makes sense that students should learn how to respond to uncertainty. Providing students with opportunities to learn how to respond productively to uncertainty will help prepare them for the kinds of real-world challenges they face now and will face in the future. Routine assignments fall short in this regard because they are designed to remove uncertainty, not insert it (Getzels, 1964). Further, such tasks offer limited opportunities for student initiative, or what motivational researchers call *agentic engagement* (Cheon & Reeve, 2015; Reeve & Tseng, 2011). Agentic engagement refers to students proactively contributing to their own learning and instruction by, for instance, identifying problems they want to solve and coming up with their own ways of solving them.

Not much of what students learn and do in school relates to actual problem solving. If you already know how to move from *A* to *Z*, then you don't have a problem; you have an exercise (Robertson, 2017) or, at best, a "pseudo-problem" (Getzels, 1964). A problem is not a problem unless it involves some level of uncertainty. The more uncertainty, the more complex the problem.

It may seem as if we are caught between two opposing aims. On the one hand, routine tasks play an important role in helping students learn academic subject matter, but they don't provide opportunities to engage with uncertainty. On the other hand, real problems encourage students to deal with the unknown, but we can't simply throw our students into the deep waters of complex challenges and hope that they will somehow learn to swim by themselves.

What's in This Book

What if we could provide opportunities for students to respond productively to uncertainty in the context of a structured and supportive learning environment? And what if we could use the routine tasks of school to prepare students to engage with more complex challenges in the classroom and beyond?

This book takes on the challenges issued in these two questions, providing the insights and tools necessary to help your students respond productively to uncertainty in a range of challenges both inside and outside the classroom.

The book is organized into two parts. Part 1 focuses on how classroom challenges can complement and serve as a warm-up for more complex, beyond-classroom challenges. The chapters in Part 1 discuss the nature and basic structure of challenges, how challenges can range in complexity, the importance of providing students with a structured and supportive learning environment, and principles that you and your students can use to design and solve complex challenges. Part 1 concludes with a chapter that introduces *lesson unplanning*, a process you can use to transform existing routine exercises into more complex classroom challenges.

The chapters in Part 2 introduce a powerful form of complex challenge known as *legacy challenges*. Legacy challenges are shot through with uncertainty because they require students to identify a problem, establish an argument for why it matters, develop a solution for addressing the problem (in collaboration with outside partners), and establish a plan to ensure that their work makes a lasting and positive contribution. Despite their complexity and scope, legacy challenges adhere to the basic framework of any challenge and require a structured and supportive learning environment. Legacy challenges represent an ideal vehicle for unleashing student problem solving because they continually drive students to encounter and respond to uncertainty. Chapters 5 through 11 include detailed sample activities and protocols that you can use to guide your students through such challenges.

The book concludes with an appendix of frequently asked questions. In addition, blank versions of some of the forms included throughout this book can be downloaded at http://www.ascd.org/ASCD/pdf/books/Beghetto2018forms.pdf.

Taken together, the ideas, tools, and activities presented in this book provide an accessible and practical approach for using complex challenges as a vehicle for students to engage with uncertainty. Doing so will help ensure that students like my daughter move away from viewing school as a worksheet factory and toward seeing it as an opportunity to develop their capacity to successfully deal with the complex challenges they face in school and beyond.

* * *

Part 1

Challenges: From Simple to Complex

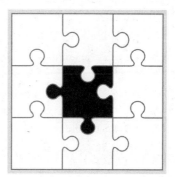

What Is a Challenge?

What if there was a way to unleash your students' problem solving by using challenges to invite good uncertainty into your classroom?

A challenge literally means an *invitation* or a *call to action*. Challenges vary in scope and complexity. When you ask students to complete academic assignments or tasks, you are presenting them with *classroom challenges,* which can range from simple to complex. When you invite students to engage with larger problems facing them, their school, the community, or beyond in ways that require them to push their learning beyond the walls of the classroom, you are presenting them with *beyond-classroom challenges*, which are invariably complex.

Although classroom and beyond-classroom challenges differ in several key ways, they share the same basic structure. Understanding this structure will enable you and your students to identify the kinds of challenges you already use and prepare you to design and implement increasingly complex challenges.

The Basic Structure of Challenges

There are four basic features that all challenges share, regardless of whether they are simple or complex, classroom or beyond-classroom challenges. I like to envision this four-part structure as a puzzle (see Figure 1.1).

Here's a rundown of the four parts of this framework:

- The **problem** is the task, question, or issue students will address or solve.
- The **process** is the approach, method, or procedure students will use to solve the problem or complete the task.

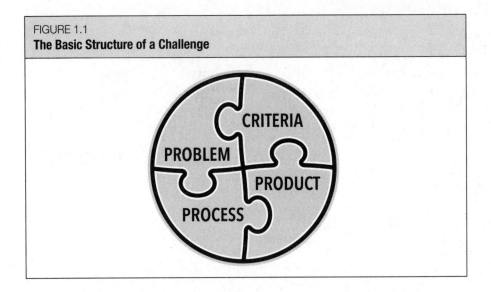

FIGURE 1.1
The Basic Structure of a Challenge

- The **product** is the solution, outcome, or demonstration of solving the problem.
- The **criteria** are the guidelines, rules, and standards for evaluating success.

If you use this basic architecture as a lens for viewing your existing assignments and tasks, you will start to recognize how those assignments align with these four features and see differences between simpler and more complex challenges. For example, let's consider a routine assignment in language arts:

> Read the assigned text and demonstrate your comprehension of the central ideas that the author is trying to communicate. Use the strategies that you were taught for identifying central ideas. Provide a written description of the central ideas and use descriptive examples from the text to justify your claims.

Figure 1.2 breaks down this assignment into the four core features of a challenge.

Note that all the components of this challenge have been determined before it's been assigned to students. This would be considered a simple classroom challenge—not because it is necessarily easy for students to complete, but because the amount of uncertainty has been minimized. Remember: *the more uncertainty students face, the more complex the challenge is.*

Now, let's take a look at a complex beyond-classroom challenge. It represents an example of the legacy challenges introduced and discussed in Chapters 5 through 11:

> A group of bilingual high school students recognize that Spanish-speaking members of their community are not receiving key health, educational, or

FIGURE 1.2

Example of a Simple Classroom Challenge

Topic: Central ideas of a story

Subject area(s): Language arts

Full challenge statement:
Read the assigned text and demonstrate your comprehension of the central ideas that the author is trying to communicate **[problem]**. Use the strategies you were taught for identifying central ideas **[process]** (e.g., *What is the topic? What does the title tell you? Which ideas in the introduction and conclusion seem to be most important? What clues can you find in the headings and subheadings? What other hints do you see of the writer's purpose, such as repeated ideas and comparisons with other topics and ideas? Can you quickly summarize the central ideas in a few words and provide a few brief examples, or do you feel like you are getting bogged down in too much general information?*). Provide a written description of the central ideas **[product]** and use descriptive examples from the text to justify your claims **[criteria]**.

Feature	Definition	Description
Problem	The task, question, or issue students will address or solve	Read the assigned text and demonstrate your comprehension of the central message of that text.
Process	The approach, strategies, or procedure students will use to solve the problem or complete the task	Use the strategies you were taught.
Product	The solution, outcome, or demonstration of solving the problem	Provide a written description of the central message.
Criteria	The guidelines, rules, and standards for evaluating success	Use descriptive examples from the text to justify your claim.

community-based information. In response, they partner with local community agencies, businesses, and the school's Languages, Business, and Technology programs to develop a student-run translation service for members of the community. Students successfully maintain an operations plan (for running the service) and a succession plan (to pass the service on to incoming juniors and seniors) and provide timely and high-quality translation services to their community (as measured by satisfaction surveys).

Although this beyond-classroom challenge, broken down in Figure 1.3, is rather complex, it contains the same core features as the simpler language arts assignment.

The key difference between these two challenges is the degree of uncertainty they present. The language arts challenge is a routine academic exercise (Robertson, 2017). All of its features are predetermined and designed without student input.

FIGURE 1.3
Example of a Complex Beyond-Classroom Challenge

Topic: Community translation service

Subject area(s): Spanish, entrepreneurship, web design

Full challenge statement:
A group of bilingual high school students recognize that Spanish-speaking members of their community are not receiving key health, educational, or community-based information **[problem]**. In response, they partner with local community agencies, businesses, and the school's Languages, Business, and Technology programs to develop a student-run translation service **[process]** for members of the community **[product]**. Students successfully maintain an operations plan (for running the service) and a succession plan (to pass the service on to incoming juniors and seniors) and provide timely and high-quality translation services to their community (as measured by satisfaction surveys) **[criteria]**.

Feature	Definition	Description
Problem	The task, question, or issue students will address or solve	Help members of the community who are not receiving key health, educational, or community-based information.
Process	The approach, method, or procedure students will use to solve the problem or complete the task	Partner with local community agencies, businesses, and the school's Languages, Business, and Technology programs to develop a student-run translation service.
Product	The solution, outcome, or demonstration of solving the problem	The student-run translation service ensures that key information is translated and made available to community members.
Criteria	The guidelines, rules, and standards for evaluating success	Students successfully maintain an operations plan (for running the service) and a succession plan (to pass the service on to incoming juniors and seniors) and provide timely and high-quality translation services to their community (as measured by satisfaction surveys).

Moreover, once students complete the assignment, the challenge is over. By contrast, the core components of the translation service challenge are not known in advance; students must face the uncertainty of identifying the problem and then developing a way to address it (Beghetto, 2017a). Even once completed, the challenge lives on in the form of a community-based translation service that is passed from one group of students to the next.

Note that both of these challenges are designed and implemented in the context of a structured and supportive learning environment. Providing this context is particularly important with more complex challenges. But how can teachers go about blending uncertainty with a supportive structure? The first step is to recognize that there are two types of uncertainty.

Good Versus Bad Uncertainty

In the context of the classroom, there is *good uncertainty* and there is *bad uncertainty* (Beghetto, 2016a). As Figure 1.4 illustrates, good uncertainty provides an opportunity to engage with an open-ended problem or a complex challenge in the context of a supportive and structured learning environment. By contrast, bad uncertainty emerges from learning experiences that confront students with uncertainty but fail to provide the necessary support and structure.

Although complex challenges by design do not have predetermined procedures or outcomes, students still need guidance to navigate the uncertainty they face along the way. In situations creating bad uncertainty, students have no idea what is expected of them, how to get started, or whether, when, or how they will receive support. Asking students to tackle the uncertainties of complex challenges or open-ended problems in the context of an unstructured learning environment invites chaos into your classroom (Reeve, 2009), creating a double whammy of uncertainty that could easily overwhelm even the most accomplished problem solvers (Beghetto, 2017b). Fortunately, this need not be the case.

You can minimize bad uncertainty and maximize good uncertainty by presenting challenges in a supportive and structured environment. First, actively monitor how students are experiencing the challenges you have designed for them. In some cases, you may quickly recognize that students are experiencing bad uncertainty. Common signs include visible frustration, confusion, and misunderstanding (Gettinger & Kohler, 2006). You might, for instance, notice that the majority of your students are no longer paying attention or that even the

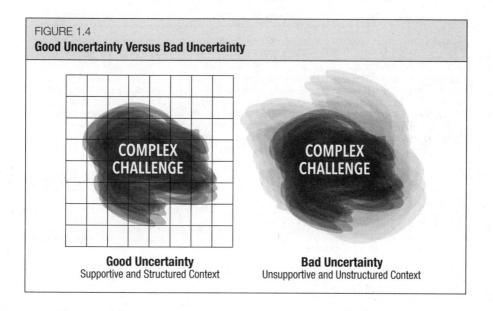

FIGURE 1.4
Good Uncertainty Versus Bad Uncertainty

Good Uncertainty
Supportive and Structured Context

Bad Uncertainty
Unsupportive and Unstructured Context

students who typically engage with learning tasks are becoming frustrated and distracted and giving up. In such cases, it is important to . . .

1. **Stop.** ("Let's stop for a moment.")
2. **Check in with students.** ("I'm noticing that several of you seem frustrated or confused by this assignment.")
3. **Address the situation.** ("Let's talk about what might not be clear or what seems confusing.")

Stopping in the middle of a lesson or an activity may seem awkward, but being able to spot and resolve bad uncertainty is crucial if we want students to successfully engage with complex challenges. Unless we provide students with the necessary support, they are unlikely to be willing to engage with more complex challenges, seek out assistance when necessary, or productively respond to the uncertainty they are facing.

In other cases, bad uncertainty may be more subtle and difficult to detect. Fortunately, simple formative assessment strategies (Wiliam, 2011) like entry/exit tickets and other brief check-ins can help you become aware of how students are experiencing the challenges you have designed and provide any needed supports. Figure 1.5 provides examples of before, during, and after check-ins that you can use.

FIGURE 1.5
Quick Challenge Check-Ins

Before the Challenge	During the Challenge	After the Challenge
After introducing a challenge but before students get started, take a moment to have your students indicate to you whether they are ready to start (thumbs up), have a quick clarification question (thumbs sideways), or feel lost and need more intensive help (thumbs down).	In addition to checking in with individual students or groups, periodically stop the whole class and have students again provide a quick indication of whether everything is OK (thumbs up), they are a bit unsure about what they are working on (thumbs sideways), or they feel stuck and need immediate help (thumbs down).	After students have completed their challenge, have them complete a simple checklist (digital or paper-and-pencil) to indicate their perspective on the level of challenge. You can also have them comment on what they feel they "got" and what they feel they still "need."
👍 Ready! 👍 Quick question. 👎 Help!	👍 All is well. 👍 A bit unsure . . . 👎 Stuck!	☐ Not challenging enough ☐ About right ☐ Too challenging _**Got**_ | _**Need**_

These quick check-ins will help you get a sense of how your students are doing, provide timely supports, and ensure that simple struggles do not grow into demoralizing frustrations. It's important to use these check-ins continually, even when students have successfully completed a challenge. Successful completion of one challenge doesn't necessarily mean students will feel confident taking on subsequent challenges, even ones at similar levels of complexity. Sometimes even students who have all the tools to succeed need some extra emotional and motivational support (Bandura, 1997; Rosiek & Beghetto, 2009). The only way to know how students are experiencing learning tasks and challenges is to take the time to ascertain their perceptions. Doing so will ensure that you are providing the support necessary for them to take on—rather than feel overwhelmed by—increasingly complex challenges.

Getting Started

The following principles will put you on the path of infusing more "good uncertainty" into your curriculum—and help students acclimate to it.

Use your classroom as an invitation to uncertainty.

What: Although simple challenges can help students develop their skills and their ability to put new learning to use, it is also important to invite students to engage with uncertainty. It is the uncertainty of complex challenges that unleashes student problem solving (Beghetto, 2017b).

How: Provide students with multiple opportunities to engage with classroom and beyond-classroom challenges. Subsequent chapters in this book provide specific examples of the different kinds of challenges you can present. You can design many of these challenges by making slight changes to your existing activities and assignments (see Chapter 5). By providing students with a full range of challenges, you will develop a classroom ethos that expects all students to continually challenge themselves regardless of whether they are starting at the ground level or are ready to push their learning beyond the walls of the classroom.

Explain what makes challenges simple versus complex.

What: It is important to help students understand that some challenges are more complex than others and that the more uncertainty they face in a challenge, the more complex the challenge is. The degree of certainty is the key difference between a routine task and a nonroutine problem (Getzels, 1964; Pólya, 1966; Pretz, Naples, & Sternberg, 2003; Schoenfeld, 1983).

How: First, remind students that all challenges share the same core features: problem, process, product, and criteria. Then encourage students to think about differences among various challenges *before* they start working on a challenge. You can give them a simple prompt, such as "Before working on this challenge, take a moment to consider how it is similar to or different from other challenges you have worked on. What aspects of this challenge do you need to figure out? What aspects have been provided for you?"

You can also provide students with some brief reflective questions *after* they have completed a challenge. High school teacher Christine Bland, for instance, has her students answer questions like *What am I still curious about? How can I extend my learning?* and *What possible challenge(s) can I explore to make a contribution beyond the walls of the classroom?* (Bland, personal communication, 2017).

Promote a productive struggle.

What: When used in the context of a supportive and structured learning environment, complex challenges can promote a *productive struggle,* meaning students experience a level of cognitive demand sufficient to be able to engage productively with intellectual challenges (Schoenfeld, 2015). This productive struggle falls somewhere between "spoon feeding content in bite-sized pieces and having the challenges so large that students are lost at sea" (Schoenfeld, 2015, p. 163). Indeed, research (Jang, Reeve, & Deci, 2010) has highlighted the importance of striking a "just right" balance between providing the necessary supportive structure and giving students opportunities to challenge themselves and take charge of their learning. Achieving this balance supports student engagement, persistence, and productive outcomes.

How: Recall that in "Goldilocks and the Three Bears," Goldilocks is able to find the "just right" bowl of porridge by sampling three different bowls. To promote a productive struggle in your classroom, try applying this "Goldilocks principle" to at least two specific areas: *task design* and *feedback.*

With respect to how you design learning tasks, it is important to blend clear, supportive guidelines and criteria with sufficient opportunities for students to grapple with uncertainty. Think of a learning *task* as a kind of learning *contract:* researchers (Chou, Halevy, Galinsky, & Murnighan, 2017) have found that contracts that strike a balance between sufficient structure *and* sufficient autonomy resulted in higher levels of task persistence, creative performance, problem solving, and cooperation. Such findings indicate that learning tasks that do not provide enough structure (at the cost of necessary guidance) or that provide too much specificity (at the cost of student autonomy) undermine students' motivation and performance.

The Goldilocks principle can be extended to the type of feedback you provide (Beghetto & Kaufman, 2007). When giving students feedback about their performance, it is important to strike a balance between honest appraisal (offering structured guidance on areas in need of improvement) and supportive encouragement (acknowledging what students have done well and encouraging them to take on additional challenges).

Although you may be able to anticipate the level and kinds of supportive structure your students need for tackling the uncertainty of a complex challenge, it is your students who will ultimately determine whether they are getting that "just right" blend. Consequently, it is important to frequently check in with your students (using simple methods like those outlined in Figure 1.5 and in Chapter 6) to monitor how they are experiencing the challenges you deliver. Using the Goldilocks principle in conjunction with frequent check-ins can help you ensure that you are supporting students while encouraging them to engage in a productive struggle.

* *

Summing Up

In this chapter, we looked at the structure of a challenge, how a challenge's degree of uncertainty determines its level of complexity, and the important distinction between good uncertainty and bad uncertainty. By becoming aware of the basic building blocks of a challenge, you will be in a better position to develop and introduce more complex challenges within the context of a structured and supportive learning environment. The following chapter will introduce you to a full continuum of challenges—from simple to complex—and help you identify the types of challenges you already use and start designing and incorporating more complex challenges for your students to tackle both inside and outside the classroom.

The Continuum of Challenges

What if you could use a full range of challenges with your students— from simple to complex—in any subject area or topic?

We've established that challenges presented with all pieces of the four-part structure in place—like the routine language arts assignment in Figure 1.2—involve minimal uncertainty and can therefore be considered simple challenges, whereas challenges with *to-be-determined* pieces, like the translation service project in Figure 1.3, introduce more complexity by requiring students to determine those missing pieces. Figure 2.1 depicts the full spectrum of challenges, with varying levels of complexity.

The Continuum of Challenges: A Closer Look

You likely already use different types of challenges with your students. The key to making the most of challenges is to use them in a systematic, balanced, and purposeful way throughout your curriculum. The first step is to become familiar with the different types of challenges: simple, moderately complex, and complex.

Simple Challenges

Simple challenges present students with minimal uncertainty because all the pieces are predetermined. Students know what the problem is, that there is a process for solving it, and that there is a predetermined answer. Simple challenges, however, are not necessarily *easy*. Students can struggle with these challenges, particularly early on in a lesson, when they are still developing their knowledge of the subject matter, concept, skill, or task.

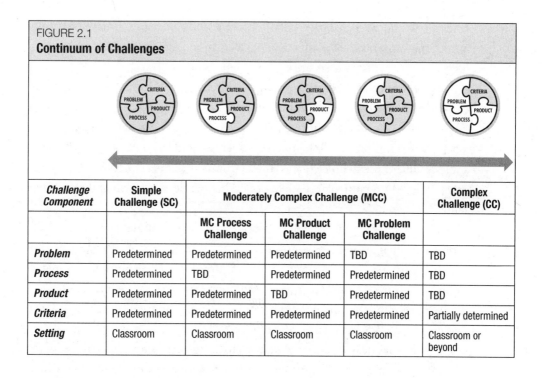

FIGURE 2.1
Continuum of Challenges

Challenge Component	Simple Challenge (SC)	Moderately Complex Challenge (MCC)			Complex Challenge (CC)
		MC Process Challenge	MC Product Challenge	MC Problem Challenge	
Problem	Predetermined	Predetermined	Predetermined	TBD	TBD
Process	Predetermined	TBD	Predetermined	Predetermined	TBD
Product	Predetermined	Predetermined	TBD	Predetermined	TBD
Criteria	Predetermined	Predetermined	Predetermined	Predetermined	Partially determined
Setting	Classroom	Classroom	Classroom	Classroom	Classroom or beyond

Simple challenges provide students with opportunities to practice newly acquired skills (e.g., "Make and record observations using the method we learned in class") and reinforce recently learned subject matter (e.g., "Identify *fore-shadowing* in these two short stories"). In the process, they also boost students' confidence in that knowledge (Lee & Anderson, 2013).

Moderately Complex Challenges

Moderately complex challenges can serve as stepping-stones to more complex challenges. As Figure 2.1 illustrates, there are at least three types of moderately complex challenges: *process, product,* and *problem* challenges.

Moderately complex *process* challenges. These problems and tasks have predetermined outcomes but offer no single or clear path for arriving at those outcomes. Instead, they confront students with the uncertainty of determining which process they will use to reach the solution.

One example of a moderately complex process challenge is a math story problem that asks students to come up with as many possible ways of arriving at the solution as they can (Niu & Zhou, 2017). With this challenge, neither you nor your students necessarily know in advance all the ways the problem can be solved. But this open-ended quality doesn't mean anything goes; you would still provide students with clear expectations and success criteria. In this case, students would need to arrive at the correct solution using a mathematically appropriate approach. Students can complete moderately complex process challenges with or without assistance.

Moderately complex *product* challenges. Moderately complex product challenges require students to use predetermined methods to address a task or situation, but the outcomes of doing so are not known in advance. An example would be having students rewrite a short story by changing some feature of their choice (e.g., removing a main character, adding a new character, or altering a particular sequence of events) while ensuring that the narrative remains coherent.

As with moderately complex process challenges, students can complete product challenges with or without assistance. In this type of challenge, the problem, process, and criteria for judging the quality of solutions are determined in advance. Consequently, even though you and your students may not know for certain what the outcome will be, your students still receive guidance and clear criteria for evaluating the results.

Moderately complex *problem* challenges. Moderately complex problem challenges require students to develop their own problem, which would have a predetermined solution and a predetermined method for arriving at that solution. An example of this type of challenge would be providing a historical outcome (e.g., a war between two countries) and asking students to describe the problem that led to that outcome using previously learned historical causal factors. Another example would be giving students a product, such as .18, and then inviting them to design as many problems as they can that would result in that product (e.g., .9 × .2 and .3 × .6) (Levenson, 2011). As with the other moderately complex challenges, these can be completed with or without teacher assistance.

Complex Challenges

Complex challenges do not have clear-cut solutions or predefined methods for arriving at those solutions. Moreover, students are expected to identify the problem, develop and test ways to productively respond to the problem, and monitor progress along the way. Complex challenges, therefore, serve as a powerful vehicle for students to practice responding to uncertainty.

Although a complex challenge lacks a predetermined problem, process, and product, it should have a structure, which includes clear guidelines and criteria for success (e.g., time constraints, directions, required academic content to be covered). Some complex challenges start out with only partially determined criteria, which become more clearly defined as the problem, process, and product begin to take shape.

How might this look in your classroom? Imagine that your students are working on a complex challenge that requires them to identify a problem to solve in their community. Although you have set timelines and other nonnegotiable criteria (e.g., project duration, project focus or scope), you need to wait to add additional criteria until after students have selected and started working on the problem they plan to solve. In this way, the problem shapes the criteria. If students, for instance, are planning a fund-raiser for a local homeless shelter, then the amount of money they need to raise to cover costs is a criterion that would become more clearly defined along the way.

Complex challenges can be designed for use either in or beyond the classroom. A look at both classroom and beyond-classroom challenges follows.

Complex classroom challenges tend to focus on helping students reinforce and apply their knowledge of academic subject matter. Such a challenge could ask students to do anything from designing their own experiments and methods for conducting those experiments to writing their own fictional narratives by deciding which style, blend of literary techniques, and elements of the story they will use.

Typically, complex classroom challenges are limited to one subject area or to a specific topic within a subject area (e.g., calculating the perimeter of a polygon). Because they also tend to be brief in duration, they can be "stacked" on top of simple and moderately complex challenges to incrementally add complexity to learning tasks and assignments.

For example, a math teacher could initially have students use a taught procedure to complete a typical practice exercise (simple challenge). Once students have built their competence with that exercise, they can move on to solve similar problems using different procedures (moderately complex challenge) and, eventually, design their own problems that can be solved using various procedures (complex challenge). Once students have confidently completed a complex classroom challenge, they can build on their knowledge by designing an even more complex challenge that calls on them to put their learning to use beyond the walls of the classroom—for example, developing a business that requires them to design and sell small-box gardens for apartment dwellers.

In this way, classroom challenges help students develop their confidence and competence working with differing levels of uncertainty, which, in turn, prepares them to engage with even more complex beyond-classroom challenges.

Complex beyond-classroom challenges have students apply and develop their knowledge of how to address complex and open-ended problems that go beyond the walls of the classroom (Beghetto, 2016b, 2017a). Such challenges can include anything from developing an app to help people locate clean water sources to coordinating an effort to provide food and clothing to homeless youth in the community.

Although beyond-classroom challenges are focused on addressing student-identified real-world problems, they can build on what students have learned (see Chapter 6). They also require students to learn new concepts and skills, which may not be anticipated in advance of the challenge. If, for instance, students are presenting a plan to the city council to offer a new activity at the town recreation center, then they need to learn how to develop a formal proposal, including a line-item budget.

Chapters 5 through 11 provide tips, guidelines, and activities to ensure that you provide the necessary support and structure for your students to launch beyond-classroom challenges.

A Word About Overwhelming (and Underwhelming) Challenges

Any challenge can become overwhelming for students if the supportive structure is lacking or if students are not yet capable of engaging with the problem. In such cases, students will need more direct instructional support and additional practice with simpler challenges to move forward.

That said, it is important to resist the temptation to too quickly characterize a challenge as overwhelming before your students have had a chance to productively struggle with it. Allowing students to engage with uncertainty, share their ideas and perspectives, and experience the limits of their current capabilities can provide you with important insights into the kinds of supports and challenges they need. Experiencing these limits in the context of a supportive learning environment can also help students develop metacognitive awareness of their strengths and limitations in light of a particular task or challenge (Kuhn, 2000; Schraw, 1998). And sometimes, all students need to work through a challenge is sufficient encouragement and emotional support (Fulmer & Turner, 2014; Rosiek & Beghetto, 2009).

It can be difficult to know what students are capable of doing until they are given an opportunity to try. Consider Brandon, an elementary student in a "low math group" who was featured in a video segment of a multi-year, classroom-based study led by Carolyn Maher and her team of researchers from Rutgers University (Harvard-Smithsonian Center for Astrophysics [HSCA], 2000). Brandon and his peers were working on "pizza problems" and encouraged to come up with their own way of representing the solution to this question: *How many different pizza choices do customers have if they can select from four toppings?*

The students came up with various ways to represent the solutions using objects and drawings. Brandon surprised the researchers and his teachers alike by coming up with a unique and elegant binary table that clearly and accurately represented the solution. As Maher explained, "Children surprise us. They have wonderful ideas. They can represent their ideas in very interesting ways, in ways that would not even have occurred to us."

This is not to say that you should require students to engage with challenges you know will overwhelm them; rather, help students recognize that if they become overwhelmed when working through a challenge, they can still benefit from the experience—as long as it is viewed as a learning opportunity (as opposed to a demoralizing failure). As Maher noted, "Unless you know what [students'] ideas are, you're not going to know what the appropriate intervention is, what the next step is, what the question is that you should be asking. Where to take that idea, to help the understanding grow for that child" (HSCA, 2000).

Sometimes, students find that a challenge is too easy. Such cases provide another good opportunity to build students' metacognitive awareness; encourage students to recognize where they stand and seek out more complex challenges if necessary. Doing so will help them develop important self- and situational knowledge.

It's safe to assume that students will sometimes feel overwhelmed and other times feel underwhelmed by the challenges they face. It's important to ensure that as students work through different types of challenges, they recognize that part of developing their competence as skilled problem solvers is to know when they need to seek out assistance and when they are ready to push on to increasingly complex challenges.

Getting Started

The following principles will help you and your students jump in and purposefully engage with increasingly complex challenges.

Trust yourself and your students.

What: It can feel risky to engage students in complex challenges, and it's normal to have concerns about stepping into uncertainty, but that should not stop you from doing so. The key is to trust yourself and your students to establish a classroom environment that supports this form of risk taking. Encourage students to let you know when a challenge is too overwhelming for them and to seek out a more challenging task when the current one is not challenging enough.

How: The most powerful way you can help students recognize and express when they need to take a step back to a simpler challenge or step up to a more complex challenge is by modeling. Like modeling academic skills and processes, modeling sensible risk taking and metacognitive awareness can reinforce and encourage those behaviors in students. Allow students to see your thinking when you are struggling ("This is not how I intended the lesson to go; let's stop for a moment and discuss what we might try differently"), and let them know when you are taking sensible risks ("I want us to try this new app for sharing ideas; this is the first time I have used it, and it may not work, but let's give it a try and then discuss it").

Monitor confidence and performance.

What: Providing students with a full continuum of challenges can help them recognize that despite similarities in structure, challenges often have significant differences that can affect students' confidence and performance. For example, a student who can easily complete complex challenges in math may not be able to successfully solve complex challenges in history, or even in certain subtopics within math. You can help students become more self-directed learners by teaching them to monitor and develop healthy and accurate confidence beliefs (Bandura, 1997) about their ability to successfully complete complex challenges within and across topics.

How: One of the best ways to determine which challenges make sense for your students or the topic you're teaching is to simply try out different types of challenges and have students take a moment to reflect on and record their experiences with these challenges.

In addition to using the quick check-ins presented in Figure 1.5 (p. 12), you can have students keep track of their confidence and performance across different challenges. Using paper and pencil, a simple polling app (e.g., Poll Everywhere), or some other record-keeping tool, you can have students record and monitor their confidence in addressing particular challenges prior to and after working on the challenge.

You can help students record and monitor their confidence and performance over time using a simple combination of a *confidence question* and a *performance question*. A simple confidence question, which students complete prior to the challenge, might look like this (adapted from Bandura, 2006):

On a scale of 0 to 100 (0 = not at all confident; 100 = completely confident), how confident are you that you can successfully complete this challenge?

Your confidence (0–100):

A simple performance question, which students answer after having engaged with the challenge, might look like this:

How did you do on the challenge? (Select one and explain.)

☐ I was successful and I'm ready for a more complex challenge.

☐ I was successful, but I want more practice with this kind of challenge.

☐ I didn't finish, but I could have with more time.

☐ I didn't finish because I need more help.

☐ I felt lost and need a lot more help.

Depending on your goals, you can develop finer-grain confidence questions for students to use and keep track of their confidence, such as the following:

On a scale of 0 to 100 (0 = not at all confident; 100 = completely confident), how confident are you that you can

• Come up with at least three of your own problems to solve?

• Come up with at least two different ways of solving this problem?

• Come up with at least two different solutions to this problem?

You can also develop deeper performance questions, such as the following:

• What aspects of this challenge did you do well on?

• What aspects of this challenge did you struggle with?

• Is there anything you need more help with?

• Are you ready to take on a more complex challenge?

Recording and reflecting on this kind of information not only helps you see how students perceive their confidence in relation to their performance but also helps students think more systematically about the relationship between their confidence and their performance. By cultivating healthy confidence beliefs, students will likely be more willing to engage with challenges, put forth and sustain effort, and seek out increasingly complex challenges and tasks (Bandura, 1997).

• •

Summing Up

In this chapter, we looked at the continuum of challenge types: simple, moderately complex, and complex. When presenting students with complex challenges, it is not always possible to predict whether a challenge will become overwhelming or not be challenging enough. By understanding that there is a full continuum of challenges that you can make available to your students, you will be in a better position to shift to simpler challenges when students get overwhelmed or increase the complexity when students are ready.

The next chapter introduces four basic action principles to help students respond productively to the uncertainty of complex challenges both inside and outside the classroom.

The Four Action Principles: Stop-Think-Do-Learn

What if you and your students learned how to use four basic action principles to respond more productively to the uncertainty of complex challenges both inside and outside the classroom?

Uncertainty is what makes a challenge a challenge. In this chapter, we explore four action principles—*stop, think, do,* and *learn*—that can help you and your students resolve the uncertainty of almost any challenging problem, situation, or task. These action principles are particularly important for addressing the complex legacy challenges discussed in Part 2 of this book.

The four principles are rooted in nearly a century of work in creative problem solving (Mumford & McIntosh, 2017; Sawyer, 2012; Wallas, 1926) and are also reflected in more recent approaches to solving complex challenges (Beghetto, 2016a), such as design thinking (Brown, 2009). (Elsewhere [Beghetto, 2016a] I describe how instructional leaders can use a version of these principles—*sit with uncertainty, engage in possibility thinking, prune possibilities,* and *take measured action*—to address uncertain situations in their own learning, leadership, and lives.) Here, I have tailored the action principles so that teachers and students can use them to tackle complex challenges in and out of the classroom.

The Four Action Principles

The four action principles used to productively respond to uncertainty are illustrated in Figure 3.1. Each of these action principles has two associated sub-actions. For instance, *stop*—the first action principle—involves *exploring* the problem and *preparing* to address it. However, I recommend focusing on the main action principles when introducing the approach to students to avoid

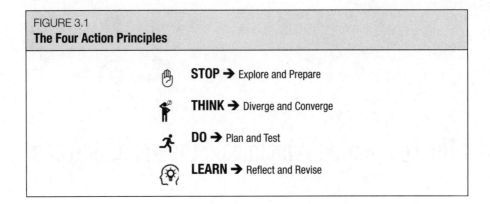

FIGURE 3.1
The Four Action Principles

STOP ➔ Explore and Prepare

THINK ➔ Diverge and Converge

DO ➔ Plan and Test

LEARN ➔ Reflect and Revise

overwhelming them and ensure that the main concepts are rooted in their memories. You can reinforce the sub-actions in the instructions and guidelines you provide to students when embarking on complex challenges.

Uncertainty serves as the catalyst for putting the four principles into action. In the context of the classroom, uncertainty can be *presented* (i.e., you use lesson unplanning to design a classroom challenge that requires students to come up with their own problems, processes, or solutions) or *found* (i.e., you challenge students to find an open-ended problem, issue, or task to define and address).

In the following sections, I describe each action principle, explain how it can be used to address complex challenges and open-ended problems, and provide checklists to reinforce the principles and their associated sub-actions. Threaded throughout is a case study of Blackawton Primary School that illustrates how the four principles look in action.

Stop

"Stop" may seem like a paradoxical first action to take when facing uncertainty, but stopping is, in fact, an action. Stopping, or sitting with the uncertainty of a problem, is one of the most important yet most frequently overlooked principles of solving complex challenges (Beghetto, 2016a; Mackworth, 1965). A major reason this step is ignored is that most people want to quickly rid themselves of any uncertainty they face.

But if students don't learn how to *stop* to explore and prepare for a challenge, they can quickly feel overwhelmed by uncertainty, which can result in a host of unproductive responses such as avoiding the problem, giving up too quickly, or trying to force-fit solutions. Help students realize that stopping is a crucial step to take when confronted with a complex challenge. Stopping allows them to carefully consider the challenge they are facing, explore the uncertainty of the challenge, and prepare themselves to address it. Let's look at the sub-actions *explore* and *prepare*.

Stop ➜ Explore. Taking time to explore a challenge instead of immediately jumping in and trying to solve it is what distinguishes expert problem solvers from beginners (Lesgold, 1988). This is because "successful insights can require a great deal of preparation and verification" (Davidson, 2003, p. 161).

The importance of this step is also illustrated in a classic study, described in Getzels and Csikszentmihalyi (1966), in which a team of researchers studied the problem-solving behaviors of students from the Art Institute of Chicago. They presented 31 art students with an authentic complex challenge. First, they provided the students with various objects to arrange and draw. Students could select as many or as few objects as they wished, arrange (and rearrange) the objects in whatever way they wanted, take as much time as they felt they needed to work on the arrangement, and then produce a drawing that satisfied their own personal standards. The researchers found that the student drawings rated as "most original" and "artistically most valuable" by a panel of art experts "were the ones produced by students who handled the most objects, explored the objects they handled most closely, and selected the most unusual objects to work with during the pre-drawing, problem-formulating period" (p. 34).

The results of this early study highlight the value of taking time to stop and explore a problem. These results also align with a long-standing belief that successful problem solvers tend to investigate a problem "in all directions" (Wallas, 1926, p. 38) prior to attempting to solve it. Encouraging students to develop the habit of stopping to explore the uncertainty they face can help prepare them to approach the problem in a more effective way.

Stop ➜ Prepare. Preparing involves clarifying what students already know about the problem, what they might need to know, and how they might engage with it. The amount of preparation time needed will vary depending on the type of challenge students are working on (Csikszentmihalyi & Sawyer, 1995; Davidson, 2003). Less complex challenges tend to require less preparation, whereas more complex ones tend to require more time and support.

One way to help students stop to explore and prepare for a complex challenge is to provide them with a quick checklist like the one in Figure 3.2. This set of reminders encourages them to slow down and take the time necessary to engage in new ways of thinking about the problem.

FIGURE 3.2
Stop: Exploring and Preparing

Stop
Do not try to solve this challenge until you have spent some time exploring and preparing for it.

Explore	Prepare
☑ What do I already know about this challenge? ☑ What kind of challenge is this? ☑ What am I being asked to do? ☑ Is there one way of solving this challenge, or are there many ways? ☑ Is there one solution, or are there many possible solutions? ☑ What are the rules, requirements, and criteria for solving this challenge? ☑ What don't I know about this challenge? ☑ What is missing from this challenge?	☑ How can I find out more about this challenge? ☑ What kind of information might I need to solve this challenge? ☑ Where can I find the information I need? ☑ Who can help me think about this problem in different ways? ☑ Who can support me in solving this problem if I get stuck? ☑ What ideas do I already have about how to work on this challenge? ☑ How would I describe this challenge to someone else? ☑ What are some first steps I might take to work through this challenge? ☑ Am I ready to start thinking about solutions, or do I need more time to explore this challenge?

Blackawton Primary School

At Blackawton Primary School in Devon, England, a group of 25 children ages 8 to 10 conducted a study, in collaboration with their teacher and a visiting neuroscientist, on bee behavior (Yong, 2010). Believing their findings could make a significant contribution to the scientific literature, they wrote them up and submitted their paper for publication. After persisting through several rejections, they were able to publish their article in *Biology Letters*, the Royal Society's leading science journal.

Publishing an article in such a learned journal is a remarkable accomplishment for anyone, let alone a group of children. Remarkable outcomes, however, can come from breaking down a complex process into smaller steps and establishing a context that supports an unshakable sense of possibility thinking (Beghetto, 2016b). It starts with being willing to stop and ask *What if?*

In the case of the Blackawton students, their teacher and an external expert (a neuroscientist and parent of one of the students) helped establish the conditions necessary for tackling this complex challenge. But it was the students who ultimately decided which questions to explore, hypotheses to test, and experiments to conduct (Yong, 2010).

The first step they took involved *stopping* to explore the kinds of scientific questions they might want to investigate. They started discussing how animals see the world and eventually landed on the topic of bees. The students, their teacher, and the visiting neuroscientist stopped and considered the questions with the goal of exploring these topics rather than trying to arrive at ready-made answers. This kind of openness and curiosity—modeled and encouraged by the teacher and the neuroscientist—allowed the students to explore what they already knew (and did not know) about the topic, identify new questions that they hadn't considered before, and prepare themselves to delve deeper into those questions.

Researchers have identified this kind of openness to experience as a core feature of creative thought and action (Kaufman, 2016). You can support this openness by making sure students have sufficient time to stop and explore the uncertainty they face. Doing so will help prepare them for engaging in the kind of thinking necessary to generate and identify new possibilities.

Think

After your students have had time to sit with the problem, exploring its features and preparing to engage with it, they are ready for the next action principle: *think*. When addressing complex and open-ended challenges, we need to engage in both *divergent* thinking (i.e., learning how to think in new ways and coming up with multiple ideas) and *convergent* thinking (i.e., selecting the best of those ideas to put into action). These types of thinking have long been associated with solving nonroutine problems (Guilford, 1967). Indeed, most models of creative problem solving (Sawyer, 2012) highlight how creative solutions can result from generating multiple possibilities and then selecting the most viable ones to implement. In practice, these twin thought processes often blend together in complex ways. It is not uncommon for students to shift between divergent and convergent thought as they generate possibilities, seek out new perspectives, challenge their assumptions, and evaluate their options.

Although accomplished problem solvers may be equipped to do much of this work on their own, students will need support and guidance from their teacher and, in some cases, outside experts. Still, the only way for students to start developing these skills is to practice using them on a range of challenges, from simple to complex, both in and out of the classroom.

Think → Diverge. Divergent thinking involves viewing a challenge in new ways and generating multiple possibilities for moving toward a solution. A simple but powerful question that can help students engage in this form of thinking is *What if?* By continually asking this question, students can generate as many ideas as possible and build on and "flip" possibilities that have already been suggested (Beghetto, 2016a; see also Chapter 7).

Consider, for instance, the problem of bullying—a thorny issue that has been further complicated by the rise of social media and other digital tools. In fact, it may be tempting to view technology as the problem. But what if this assumption were flipped? What if we could make technology part of the solution?

Natalie Hampton, a teenager in California, did just that by developing an app called "Sit With Us" (National Public Radio, 2016). The app enables socially isolated students to discreetly find a place to sit in the lunchroom with peers who have posted "open lunches." Another teen, Trisha Prabhu, used technology to disrupt bullying by developing the "ReThink" app to help potential cyberbullies think twice about posting hurtful comments. The app detects unkind or malicious messages (e.g., "Go kill yourself" or "You are ugly") and gives the user a chance to reconsider the post by saying, "Hold on—that message you are about to send may be hurtful to others. Are you sure you want to post it?" (Girlshealth.gov, 2016).

These kinds of breakthroughs start with reconsidering assumptions, engaging in possibility thinking, and generating new ways of thinking about a problem. You can support this kind of thinking in your students by modeling it yourself (Beghetto, 2016a, 2016b) as well as encouraging it in them.

Think → Converge. Convergent thinking is a form of evaluative thinking that helps students review the ideas and possibilities they have generated via divergent thinking and home in on those that seem most viable. This is a learned process, and your students likely will need encouragement and guidance to make sure that they evaluate *all* possibilities, including those that seem rock solid, those that seem weak, and those that fall somewhere in between.

Without taking the time to look at all ideas with a critical eye, students may miss out on some great possibilities (Bilalić, McLeod, & Gobet, 2008). Encourage them to open their minds, explore both familiar and strange ways of doing things, and challenge their assumptions and first impressions. As an exercise, you might have students identify product ideas that most people initially dismissed as silly or faddish but that ended up yielding millions in sales (Graham, 2010), such as bottled water or Pet Rocks.

Another good way for students to practice convergent thinking is to evaluate and provide feedback on their peers' ideas—with a focus on improving, not ripping apart, these ideas. I recommend establishing guidelines to ensure that student feedback is both honest and supportive (see Figure 7.1 on p. 79 for an example of ground rules for sharing). To make sure students offer *and* receive feedback constructively, consider having them preface feedback with the words *what if* (Beghetto, 2016a). By framing feedback this way, you and your students offer open-ended possibilities rather than closed-off criticisms.

For example, instead of saying, "That isn't a new idea; you need to come up with a different one," try, "What if you put a new twist on that idea to make it your own?" Rather than say, "Homeroom teachers already provide an orientation to 6th graders on the first day of middle school," ask, "What if instead of having teachers do the orientation, we let 6th graders run it?"

When students learn how to provide honest and helpful feedback to their peers, they experience the added benefit of learning how to generate better ideas themselves. Indeed, researchers (Gibson & Mumford, 2013) have found that people who know how to evaluate others' ideas tend to be better at coming up with good solutions themselves.

The checklist in Figure 3.3 provides some initial prompts to guide students as they generate and evaluate ideas for tackling complex challenges.

FIGURE 3.3
Think: Diverging and Converging

Think
Take time to come up with numerous possibilities, and then select the best ones.

Diverge	Converge
☑ What are all the different ways you can come up with to solve this challenge? ☑ Try to come up with an idea that no one else will think of. What is that idea? ☑ What if you flipped some of the ideas you have about the problem? What might happen? ☑ How can you view this challenge from a different perspective? ☑ Think of a few different people—you can choose people you know or famous people, alive or dead. How might these people view this challenge? ☑ What if you did an idea mash-up, combining your ideas with a classmate's? ☑ Keep asking *What if?*	☑ Take the time to consider all your ideas, no matter how silly or unusual they seem. ☑ Which idea or solution do you like best? ☑ How might you make your weak ideas stronger? ☑ Can you find a weakness in the idea that you think is the strongest? ☑ Share your ideas with a partner. What does he or she have to say about your ideas? ☑ Give feedback on someone else's ideas. Make sure you provide specific and helpful feedback for making his or her ideas even better. How does providing feedback to others help you think differently about your own ideas? ☑ Whom else might you ask to provide feedback on your ideas? Is there someone you know who is an expert in this area? ☑ Of all the ideas you have developed, which ones do you think will work best in solving this challenge?

Blackawton Primary School

After the Blackawton Primary students explored and prepared to delve into how animals—specifically, bees—see the world, they were ready to engage in divergent thinking around the problem. They thought about bee behavior like playing a game of Sudoku or solving a puzzle. After thinking more about games and puzzles, they started asking more specific questions about bees and whether bees might learn to solve puzzles.

Next, they started to converge their thinking and eventually arrived at the question of how bees decide which flowers to collect nectar from and which flowers to avoid (i.e., flowers they'd already collected nectar from or flowers that might be bad for them). By thinking more deeply about this question, they further narrowed their focus to consider whether bees might learn to use the spatial relationships between colors—just like a puzzle—to decide which flowers to visit (Blackawton et al., 2011; Yong, 2010).

When you support students in engaging in divergent thinking, you put them in a position to produce and explore multiple possibilities. Doing so requires them to rethink assumptions and explore questions from various perspectives. The *think* phase, however, is not simply about generating ideas. Students also need to start focusing their thinking, narrowing down the possibilities, and converging on those that seem most viable to pursue. By supporting students in these efforts, you will help ensure that they are ready to start acting on those possibilities.

 Do

Once students have generated and selected a few possibilities, it's time to act on those ideas. This is what the *do* principle is all about. No matter how promising an idea is, unless students act on it, its potential remains dormant. To make their idea come to life, students need to develop a plan of action and then test it out.

Do → Plan. Prior to testing out an idea, it is important for students to plot out the steps they will take. This includes reviewing and clarifying the criteria for success.

When working on a smaller-scale classroom challenge, this planning phase might be quite short, simply involving students familiarizing themselves with the predetermined criteria of the challenge. For example, middle school French students who are tasked with developing and printing their own modern French restaurant menu would need to double-check the set criteria to make sure that their ideas for appetizers, entrées, and desserts adhere to the requirements of the challenge. Prior to printing out their final menu, they would also need to plan a way to test the layout of their design to ensure that it fits within the allotted space constraints.

Although the planning phase for a more ambitious beyond-classroom challenge would take a bit more time, the focus should still be on planning a series of small, measurable actions that align with the criteria for success. This not only prevents students from becoming overwhelmed but also enables them to monitor progress and make on-the-fly adjustments (Beghetto, 2016a). Making gradual but consistent progress is also a powerful way to build up confidence and persistence (Amabile & Kramer, 2011).

The goal of this phase is for students to develop quick and easy ways to test out their ideas and solutions against some pre-established criteria for success. Students may need assistance from you or outside partners to clarify and, in some cases, develop these criteria. You can do this by helping students list some simple indicators of success that they can monitor.

If, for instance, they are planning an annual cooking competition between teachers and students to raise money for a local food pantry, you can have them calculate how much money they need to raise through ticket sales to cover their food costs and make a profit. The metrics need not be complex, just relevant to helping them monitor their plan's effectiveness. Depending on the problem, it may be one simple indicator (e.g., the amount of money to be raised) or multiple indicators (e.g., the number of people attending the event, the number of people who return to subsequent events, the number of events hosted throughout the year, the number of new events launched in other communities, and so on).

Do ➜ Test. Once students have a plan of action, they are ready to test out their ideas. These should be small tests. Depending on the challenge, students might first share their ideas with other people, either in or out of the classroom. In other cases, they might want to develop a pilot or prototype. The goal is to test out ideas and determine whether they are making progress toward solving the challenge or going off track. This type of progress monitoring is particularly important when working on larger-scale challenges.

For instance, students who plan to establish a volunteer-based restorative justice program in their school would want to test it out on a small scale. The key criteria, in this case, would be whether a pilot run of the program would result in more students being willing to sign up as mediators and participants in the next iteration of the program.

Entrepreneurs who are in the process of launching their own start-ups are essentially facing a complex challenge. One popular idea for tackling such a challenge is to develop a *minimum viable product,* or MVP (Ries, 2011). An MVP is a way to test out a potential product or solution in a way that provides actionable information for product improvement with minimal cost to the company. An MVP could be anything from a video that describes a product to a comprehensive test of a service with just one customer to get an in-depth look at the full process. At the school level, 7th graders who are making and selling soap shaped like circuit boards to raise funds for new technology for the school could create a few different prototypes of the soap (e.g., with varying sizes and colors) to try selling in the school store.

Although the complex challenges you assign to students may not involve starting a business, developing a strategy for quickly testing out ideas on a small scale helps students identify strengths and address weaknesses in a timely manner. In this way, students can "fail fast to learn quickly" (Beghetto, 2016a). For example, the students creating and selling soaps might find out that their soaps disintegrate too quickly but that the multicolored versions are a hit. Both data points are immensely useful to have before they bring their "Tech-Bubbles" idea to scale.

Figure 3.4 provides a checklist of questions and prompts to guide students as they plan and test out their approaches to complex challenges.

FIGURE 3.4
Do: Planning and Testing

Do
Plan to take some small, initial steps so you can test out your ideas.

Plan	Test
☑ What are some small, initial steps you can take? ☑ How will you know if you are on the right track? ☑ What do you need to do to be successful in this challenge? ☑ Whom can you ask for help in thinking about steps you can take? ☑ Whom can you ask for help in figuring out how to know if you are on the right track?	☑ Put your ideas to the test by trying them out and checking whether they are helping you move forward in solving the challenge. ☑ What is working? What isn't working? ☑ Make sure to keep checking whether you are meeting the criteria for success. ☑ If an idea is not working, try another one. ☑ Keep testing out ideas and jot down some notes about what you have tried, what seems to be working, and what isn't working. ☑ If nothing seems to work or you get stuck, then it might be time to rethink your ideas and come up with some new alternatives.

Blackawton Primary School

Once the Blackawton students had narrowed their focus to exploring how bees learn to decide which flowers to collect nectar from, they needed to plan a way to test out their ideas. Working in collaboration with their teacher and the visiting neuroscientist, the students designed a simulated flower box to test whether bees could learn to navigate different patterns of color and location, recorded their observations, and wrote up their results. Realizing that their results might be a significant contribution to the scientific study of bee behavior, the students submitted their findings for publication in a scientific journal (Blackawton et al., 2011; Yong, 2010).

The *do* action principle drives students to bring possibilities to life. Because even the most promising ideas will be meaningless if they're not acted on (Beghetto, 2016a), the *do* phase requires students to develop a feasible plan for developing and testing out possibilities. This may require developing a prototype or running a small pilot. The key is not to get bogged down in trying to develop some highly polished beta test but, rather, to make the minimum effort necessary to yield meaningful, actionable information for product improvement according to the predetermined criteria.

Once students have planned and acted on their ideas, they will be ready to learn from their actions—even when their tests don't work out or yield surprising results.

Learn

Learning—the final action principle—inevitably involves change (Alexander, Schallert, & Reynolds, 2009). In the context of addressing a complex challenge, learning refers to discovering what does and does not work and making necessary changes. Naturally, students will learn from successfully resolving a complex challenge, but they will also learn from setbacks and failures. Although students may not be used to viewing failures as learning opportunities, you can help them see that failures often yield important information that can show them how to move forward—or indicate when it's time to move in a different direction.

For example, a team of teenagers developed a "Lean on Me" event for pregnant and parenting high schoolers (One Stone, 2016) with the goal of establishing a mutual support network among teen parents in their community. The team planned a variety of enjoyable activities aimed at building community among the invitees. But on the day of the event, none of the invited teens showed up. Although this might be viewed as a failure, the teens who planned and organized the event viewed it as "failing forward." Instead of feeling demoralized by the experience, they focused on what they could learn from it. They recognized that teen parents are very busy and may not have the time to attend events like the one they planned. The team members used the day to reflect, work together, and design gifts (e.g., mosaics, decorated diaper bags) that they donated to a local Women's and Children's Alliance center and to teen parents who attended a local high school. In the end, the team transformed the "failure" into a meaningful learning experience.

If we want students to learn from putting their ideas to the test, we need to support them and help them learn from the churn of emotions they may experience when things don't go as planned. We need to help them reflect on their experience and revise their plans accordingly.

Learn → Reflect. Reflecting on the information gathered during the *do* phase is a crucial step for successfully completing a challenge. During this step, students think about what they learned from testing their ideas and identify those ideas' strengths and weaknesses. This process requires the honest and sometimes painful work of letting go of some cherished ideas and assumptions to make room for better ones. This is especially difficult to do when better ideas are not readily available or students continue to run into roadblocks.

Failure can elicit a variety of painful emotions. Rather than try to deny or quickly justify those emotions, it can be more effective to acknowledge and allow students to experience them. Saying, "I can see how frustrated you are. It is hard to have a setback like this. Let's see what we can learn from it to help strengthen your idea" provides emotional support (Fulmer & Turner, 2014) and helps students move on and learn from setbacks. The goal is to help students reframe failure as the lever of learning rather than something to be avoided at all costs.

Letting students know that it is OK to feel frustration and other difficult emotions can boost their sense of autonomy (Reeve, 2009). Moreover, there is evidence (Nelson, Malkoc, & Shiv, 2018) that focusing on the negative *emotions* one feels following failure can be more advantageous to subsequent learning and improvement than focusing on *thoughts* (e.g., justifications for the failure). One reason for this is that negative emotions can motivate people to put forth effort to improve on past mistakes when facing similar situations (Nelson et al., 2018).

Conversely, a more cognitive focus can impede learning and improvement if the focus is on self-protecting thoughts (e.g., "That was no big deal" or "I didn't do anything wrong; it was the circumstances") rather than self-improvement (Nelson et al., 2018). Of course, focusing too much on negative emotions is not a good thing, either. If students feel shamed by a failure and believe they can't improve, then they may give up on their goals and aspirations (see Beghetto & Dilley, 2016). The key is to help students view setbacks—including the negative emotions that come with these experiences—as a normal and important part of the learning process.

Viewing failures and setbacks as learning opportunities doesn't come naturally; it takes practice. One of the best ways to help students adopt this perspective is to help them learn from setbacks and failures. Throughout the learning process, encourage your students to normalize setbacks and reframe them as learning opportunities. One way to help them anticipate setbacks is to adopt or develop a classroom motto, such as "This may not work, but we will still learn from it" (inspired by Godin, 2015).

Another way of normalizing failure as a part of the process is to look at examples of how accomplished problem solvers have worked through their own failures, rejections, and setbacks (Root-Bernstein & Root-Bernstein, 2017; Sternberg & Lubart, 1995). Accessible books, like *They All Laughed* (Flatow, 1992), provide aspirational stories about people who struggled to achieve breakthroughs when faced with complex challenges. You can also invite professionals into the classroom to discuss their own processes, including the ways they deal with failure. This can bring the process to life and help students recognize how common setbacks are.

Remember: the goal of reflection is not navel-gazing, but identifying which ideas are working and which ideas need additional work and revision.

Learn ➔ Revise. Students tend not to like revising their work. If you have ever taught writing, you likely know this all too well. Once students have completed a process or product, it is common for them to mentally check it off their list and move on to the next thing. When an assignment or test is over, most students quickly accept the grade and move on. Because they are rarely expected to revisit and revise their initial thinking, it can be difficult to persuade students to return to what they perceive as finished work.

It can be helpful to foster in students what I call a "loopback mindset." A loopback mindset represents the willingness to continually return to ideas that may have seemed solid but, after testing, clearly need to be reworked, revised, or even relinquished entirely in favor of pursuing better ones.

Again, looking at how experts deal with failure and change course to solve challenges a different way can help normalize the process of revision for students while providing models of how to approach their own setbacks (Root-Bernstein & Root-Bernstein, 2017). You can also have students discuss their own experiences with a challenge in small groups and then share their perspectives with the whole class prior to moving on to a new activity or challenge. Here are some questions students might address:

- What was something that happened during the challenge that was unexpected and required you to rethink your approach or take a different approach?
- How did that setback make you feel? What did you learn from the setback?
- If you were to do this challenge over again, what, if anything, might you do differently?

The *revise* component of learning involves carefully and critically going back over what worked and what didn't. The amount of time this takes depends on the complexity and scope of the challenge, but it is important to cultivate this habit whenever students engage with complex challenges—even those that students quickly and successfully resolve. With more complex legacy challenges, students will need multiple extended opportunities to reflect on and revise their efforts. The checklist in Figure 3.5 can help students develop these learning habits.

FIGURE 3.5
Learn: Reflecting and Revising

Learn
Reflect on and revise your ideas so you can learn from your setbacks.

Reflect	Revise
☑ It is OK to feel frustrated and upset about the ideas that didn't work. ☑ Sometimes the best solutions come from continually testing out all kinds of ideas, making changes, and trying again. ☑ It can help to talk with someone else and hear different ideas. Whom can you talk to about ideas and setbacks? ☑ What worked well when you tested out your ideas? How do you know it worked well? ☑ What didn't work well? Why do you think it didn't work? ☑ If you were to try this again, what would you do differently? What would you keep the same? ☑ How might you think about this challenge in a different way? Is there something you're missing?	☑ What changes might you make to your ideas? Try to be as specific as possible. ☑ How might you do things differently? ☑ What things might you keep the same if you try this again? ☑ If you are not sure how to make changes, whom can you ask (in or out of the classroom) for help to get back on track? ☑ If you were successful in solving the challenge, can you think of additional ways you could have solved it? Can you come up with an even better way than the one you used? ☑ If you were not successful, you may need to go back and generate some new ideas, select the ones that might work, and try those out. Be patient and keep trying. You may need to go through this process several times to move forward. ☑ Regardless of whether you were successful, what did you learn from this process?

Blackawton Primary School

When it came time for the Blackawton Primary students to try to publish their findings, their paper was rejected by several scientific journals. The editors who rejected the paper were positive about the work overall but, because of the paper's unorthodox format (e.g., it was written in "kidspeak," featured hand-drawn tables, and lacked proper scientific citations), determined that it could not be published in a scientific journal (Blackawton et al., 2011; Yong, 2010).

The students learned from this negative outcome. They reflected on their effort and decided to revise their approach by reaching out to four established experts in the field of vision and asking them to conduct a review of the paper. Only one of the four "questioned its scientific merit" (Yong, 2010); the others recognized that the paper's findings represented a worthy contribution to the field.

The students then shared these external reviews with the editor of *Biology Letters*. The editor eventually decided to publish the paper after receiving four additional positive reviews and with the stipulation that the students' paper would be published alongside two detailed scientific commentaries written by experts who could provide a more scientific context for the children's work.

The Blackawton students worked through a complex challenge using all four action principles. Their experience illustrates how this process might unfold in real life and highlights how some of the principles overlap, intersect, and repeat. The rejection of the students' paper, for instance, required them to sit with the rejection (*stop*), reflect on the setback (*learn*), consider how they might revise their approach by seeking out additional reviews (*think*), test out this new approach by submitting their findings to a different journal (*do*), and, eventually, work with the journal editor from *Biology Letters* to publish their results (*learn*).

● ●

Getting Started

The following principles will help you and your students make the *stop-think-do-learn* approach an indelible practice in your classroom.

Model *stop-think-do-learn* and make the steps explicit.

What: Just about any time you and your students face uncertainty, you can take a moment to discuss previous situations when you or they resolved uncertainty by stopping, thinking, doing, and learning.

How: Highlighting and discussing how the action principles have worked in previous situations can reinforce your students' awareness and subsequent use of the principles. You can also hang a simple *stop-think-do-learn* reminder in your classroom, write a reminder to use the principles at the top of your assignments, and encourage students to share when and how they used these steps to tackle challenges both in and out of the classroom. With enough modeling and reinforcement, using these principles will become second nature for you and your students.

Don't shy away from moving backward, forward, and everywhere in between.

What: Applying the action principles for solving complex challenges often follows the sequence presented in this chapter. As you likely recognize, however, the principles and accompanying sub-actions can and do overlap. When tackling a complex challenge, it is not uncommon for students to move back and forth between these principles and use them repeatedly even with the same problem. Cycling through the *stop-think-do-learn* process and building up an explicit awareness of how they apply the principles helps cultivate a loopback mindset.

How: When you first introduce the action principles to students, explain that although they are often used in the *stop-think-do-learn* sequence, they can also be used in different ways when working on a challenge, including moving back to earlier principles. For example, after putting ideas into action in the *do* stage, new uncertainties may emerge that compel students to return to the *stop* principle.

Invite students to think about complex challenges they have worked on in the past and try to use the *stop-think-do-learn* labels to describe the process they used to solve that challenge. You can also have them keep a "challenge journal" and have them periodically document their work on the challenges using the *stop-think-do-learn* labels. Doing so will build their awareness of how these principles look in practice and how they might use them more systematically to work through increasingly complex challenges.

Encourage and take beautiful risks.

What: Being willing to face and respond to uncertainty can feel risky—but *good* risky. I refer to this type of risk as a *beautiful* risk (Beghetto, 2017b). A beautiful risk is different from other kinds of risky behavior because the potential benefits to oneself *and* others outweigh the potential costs.

For example, riding a bicycle without a helmet is a *reckless* risk, because whatever perceived benefits there may be (e.g., "I enjoy the feeling of the wind blowing through my hair") are outweighed by the potential costs (e.g., serious head injury). By contrast, developing an after-school program to build connections among students who have trouble making friends is a beautiful risk because the potential benefits (e.g., promoting positive social relationships, experiencing the satisfaction of developing a successful solution to a problem) outweigh the costs (e.g., the time and effort invested in developing the program, possible lack of participation).

How: Complex challenges require you and your students to encourage and take beautiful risks. To cultivate a learning environment conducive to this type of risk taking, establish the expectation that all students need to take these kinds of risks. You can lay the groundwork by demonstrating an unshakeable sense of possibility thinking (Beghetto, 2016b), which involves continually asking *What if?* and building up students' resilience and willingness to learn from failures.

You and your students can discuss the kinds of sensible, beautiful risks you have taken in your own learning and lives and how they have led to positive outcomes for you and others. You can also seek out and share anecdotes illustrating beautiful risks taken by other young people as well as experts in various fields. Learning from models of sensible risk takers can increase students' willingness to take similar risks in their own learning (Bandura, 1997). Most important, make sure you consistently invite students to push themselves and take beautiful risks as they tackle increasingly complex challenges.

● ●

Summing Up

In this chapter, we explored the *stop-think-do-learn* approach that you and your students can use to tackle just about any challenge, whether simple or complex. Although each action principle's associated sub-actions help clarify the steps students must take, these processes will ultimately take shape in the context of the specific challenges that you and your students address. Help students develop a healthy habit of using these four principles whenever they face a challenging problem or task.

The following chapter introduces a process called *lesson unplanning* that will help you transform routine tasks into more challenging ones. Doing so will ensure that you have a full range of challenges to provide to students, which will be helpful when you dive into the complex beyond-classroom challenges discussed in Part 2 of this book.

4

Lesson Unplanning

What if you could transform your existing lessons, activities, and assignments into more complex ones by replacing a preplanned feature with a to-be-determined feature?

Too often, we over-plan our students' learning experiences. Although providing students with highly planned lessons does have its place, it is also important to give students opportunities to tackle uncertainty. In this chapter, I explain how you can introduce uncertainty into the tasks and assignments you already provide through a process called *lesson unplanning* (Beghetto, 2017c).

Lesson unplanning involves adding complexity to existing lessons and classroom structures by removing some of the *preplanned* features of a task or an assignment and replacing them with *to-be-determined* features. If you want to incorporate more complex challenges into your practice but don't feel comfortable diving directly into legacy challenges, lesson unplanning is a great entry point. Once you feel oriented, you can get more ambitious and begin to use complex challenges beyond the classroom.

From Planned to Unplanned

Lesson unplanning can help you provide a more balanced diet of challenges to your students, ranging from simple to complex. The process begins by selecting a topic you teach, reviewing the *planned* tasks or activities that you already use, and selecting a few that you want to transform into more complex challenges.

At this point, you'll be ready to engage in lesson unplanning. Before doing so, however, I recommend acquainting yourself with three general guidelines:

1. Start with a dead (or dreaded) lesson.
2. Get clear on the "nonnegotiables."
3. Anticipate the need for adaptive challenges.

Each guideline is discussed in the sections that follow.

Start with a Dead (or Dreaded) Lesson

A good place to start with lesson unplanning is to identify an activity or assignment you or your students dread. It can be a lesson you feel is already "dead in the water" or one that simply needs revamping. Lesson unplanning opens up new and potentially more engaging learning possibilities in what would otherwise be a tedious or ineffective exercise. In this way, your initial foray into lesson unplanning will be low-risk, with the added benefit of breathing new life into a lesson that really needs it. Starting with a lesson that you believe needs improvement will also prepare you to rethink and possibly revise some of your more cherished lessons down the line.

Get Clear on the "Nonnegotiables"

Once you have identified an activity or assignment, you'll need to take some time to get clear on the "nonnegotiables." The nonnegotiables represent the criteria piece of the challenge puzzle and include any standards you're required to meet, concepts you're not willing or able to change, and what is expected of you and your students. If you must teach a unit on the defining features of haiku poetry, for example, then it is not an option to let students work on free verse instead.

In addition to the academic standards and content the challenge must cover, it's important to consider constraints such as time and resources. If, for example, you have only one day to devote to teaching about buoyancy, you will not be able to design a two-day buoyancy challenge. This is often easier said than done, particularly when a student comes up with a compelling and meaningful way to extend the lesson. In such cases, rather than shutting down the student's initiative, you can explore ways for the student to build on this work beyond the lesson—for example, as an independent study or a project for a science fair or competition.

Determining your nonnegotiables upfront will help you design an activity or assignment that meets the constraints of your lesson. This process will also provide the necessary structure and guidelines for your students to adhere to as they engage with the uncertainty you are introducing into their learning.

Anticipate the Need for Adaptive Challenges

You likely will have some students who need a bit more practice and preparation before they are ready to tackle a new complex challenge. You may also have some students who are ready to take a challenge to the next level. It's therefore a good idea to build in enough flexibility to be able to modify a challenge by *lowering the floor* or *raising the ceiling*.

Lowering the floor. Lowering the floor of a challenge means giving students who need it a little extra help with hints, suggestions, or other supports, such as the option to practice with simple challenges prior to moving on to more complex ones. The goal of this modification is to help students who are struggling with the uncertainty of developing their own process, product, or problem get the structure and support they need to successfully engage with the challenge.

In some cases, students simply need a brief lowering of the floor to enable them to jump on board. Some students may feel initially stuck or overwhelmed by the challenge and need additional emotional or motivational support to move forward (Fulmer & Turner, 2014; Rosiek & Beghetto, 2009). Taking some time to acknowledge their frustration and giving them a few ideas and a bit more direction may be all it takes to jump-start them on the challenge.

Other students may need the floor to be lowered for a longer duration so that they can develop the basic access knowledge and skills necessary for stepping up to the challenge. No amount of encouragement will provide this foundational level of competence; these students require more direct instructional support and practice to get up to speed.

In all cases, lowering the floor doesn't mean lowering expectations; it's important to encourage productive risk taking by letting all students know that you expect them to progress to more complex follow-up challenges that you (or they) design. This can transform what might otherwise be experienced as demoralizing failure into "productive failure" (Lee & Anderson, 2013).

Raising the ceiling. Raising the ceiling means adding more complexity to a task for students who need a higher level of challenge. This may entail having students develop additional processes or alternative products or identify further problems. It may also include making the criteria more challenging by adding extra requirements to an assignment or a task.

When you raise the ceiling, you give students the opportunity to push beyond the challenges you initially provide. Working together, you and your students can further unplan some aspect of the task to increase its complexity. This might require students to come up with additional problems to address (e.g., developing extension experiments in a science lab), develop new approaches for demonstrating their understanding (e.g., identifying *foreshadowing* in various genres and narrative mediums, such as printed text versus film adaptations), or develop new products or outcomes (e.g., exploring how alternative historical circumstances might have resulted in a different historical outcome).

In some cases, students will want to continue to push on beyond the time you have allotted. As mentioned, you can encourage these students to propose a challenge that might serve as an enrichment activity or independent study project. Even if you don't have time to provide direct instructional support, you can still offer to check in with students or help connect them to outside partners who can support their work.

Lesson unplanning is an active process that continues to evolve as students engage with the challenges you provide. You will discover that some students need more structure, whereas others push for more freedom. By knowing this, and by inviting your students into the lesson unplanning process, you'll be ready to make on-the-fly modifications to the classroom challenges your students face.

Lesson Unplanning in Action

The protocol depicted in Figure 4.1 provides a step-by-step overview of how to engage in the process of lesson unplanning. Let's put these steps into action. Imagine that a 6th grade language arts teacher wanted to include some more complex challenges after teaching the topics of identifying central ideas in a text and using examples from the text to justify claims. Typically, this teacher uses various simple challenges to help students practice and apply their knowledge. As a first step toward introducing more complex challenges, the teacher uses a lesson unplanning form (see Figure 4.2) to identify which activities she will keep, modify, and replace and to sketch out the revised or brand-new activities. (A blank version of this form is available for download at http://www.ascd.org/ASCD/pdf/books/Beghetto2018forms.pdf. You can use the form to organize your process and transform activities and tasks for any topic you teach.)

After working through the unplanning guidelines, the teacher decided to keep one simple challenge as is, modify three others into moderately complex challenges, and replace one with a more complex challenge. The teacher kept worksheet 1 as is because it provides students with useful practice and "worked examples." It also serves as a good point of reference for students to return to when working on more complex problems. The teacher recognized that students would need this highly structured practice to develop the skills necessary for engaging in the more complex challenges.

FIGURE 4.1
The Lesson Unplanning Process

$\mathcal{STEP}$ (1) **Select** a topic you have already taught or plan to teach.

$\mathcal{STEP}$ (2) **Identify** the various activities and assignments you plan to use for this topic.

$\mathcal{STEP}$ (3) **Classify** the assignments as *keep, modify,* or *replace.*

 Keep
- Is this an activity or assignment I need to keep?
- Why do I need to keep it?
- Does it provide practice and rehearsal that is necessary for reinforcing and demonstrating learning?
- What might happen if I changed or replaced this assignment?

 Modify
- Is this an activity or assignment I can modify?
- Why do I feel I need to modify it?
- If I do modify it, which features do I want to keep, and which features can I change?
- What might happen if I changed or replaced this assignment?

 Replace
- Is this an activity or assignment I can replace with something new?
- Why do I feel I need to replace it?
- What are the important features of this assignment that the replacement needs to cover?
- How can I make sure that the new option will provide my students with the important features of this assignment?
- What might happen if I changed or replaced this assignment?

$\mathcal{STEP}$ (4) **Design** new versions of the assignments classified as *modify* and *replace*.

 Modify to develop a *moderately complex* or *complex challenge:*
- If I'm starting with a simple challenge, which features can I remove to make it a moderately complex or complex challenge?
- Which features do I want to keep, and which features will I change?
- Will this modification allow me to cover what is needed for this topic?

 Replace with a *moderately complex* or *complex challenge:*
- Will this replacement be a moderately complex or complex challenge?
- Will this replacement allow me to cover what is needed for this topic?

$\mathcal{STEP}$ (5) **Review** the assignments together and **revise** as necessary.

 Do I have at least one moderately complex and one complex challenge?
- If not, why not?

 Taken together, do these assignments and activities cover what is needed for this topic?
- If not, what modifications do I need to make?

FIGURE 4.2
Lesson Unplanning Form

Subject area: Language arts

Topic: *Identifying central ideas of text* and *Justifying claims with examples from the text*

Keep (K), Modify (M), or Replace (R)	Simple Challenge	Moderately Complex Challenge	Complex Challenge
(K) M R	Practice worksheet 1		
K (M) R	Practice worksheet 2	"Your own story"	
K (M) R	In-class activity 1	"Show it your way"	
K (M) R	Practice worksheet 3	"Multiple ideas"	
K M (R)	~~In-class activity 2~~		"All you!"

Notes:

- Practice worksheet 1—keep. Provides the kids with good practice and some great mini-examples that have been helpful for them to use as a reference.

- Practice worksheet 2—modify. I like the prompts of this worksheet, but rather than use the story it recommends, I'll let students identify their own story from any author (including themselves) in any medium (e.g., film, graphic novel). I want to introduce the idea that a story or "text" is not limited to the written word.

- In-class activity 1—modify. We usually read a text together, and then I ask students to individually write out the central idea and share it. This time, I'll have them represent the central idea in whatever way they want *other* than writing it individually (e.g., doing a role-play, conveying it through images, working alone or together).

- Practice worksheet 3—modify. I usually use this as follow-up homework to the in-class activity. It is essentially the same worksheet as worksheet 1, just a different text. The kids love this story, so I want to keep it, but I want to give them a chance to go beyond identifying *one* central idea and recognize that even the same reader might be able to recognize *multiple* central ideas. I want students to try to view this story from multiple perspectives and come up with various possible central ideas while still justifying their claims by using descriptive examples from the text.

- In-class activity 2—replace. I usually end this topic with an in-class activity like activity 1. I want to challenge students to bring all the pieces together and take ownership of finding a text and identifying the central idea, but also to discuss what they found most interesting about the text and why, demonstrate the central idea and what they found interesting in their own way (e.g., via images, objects, memes, or whatever they come up with), and connect it back to descriptive examples to justify their claims and interpretations.

The teacher decided to infuse uncertainty into the predetermined *problem* in worksheet 2 by having students identify their own story by any author (including themselves) and in any medium (to demonstrate that a "text" can go beyond the printed word). Next, she modified the predetermined *process* and *product* of in-class activity 1 by asking students to demonstrate the central idea of a text in a way other than writing it individually. The teacher also modified the predetermined *product* in worksheet 3 to push students to recognize that stories can have multiple ideas depending on one's perspective. Finally, the teacher replaced in-class activity 2 with a complex challenge requiring students to take charge of defining the *problem, process,* and *product* while retaining the same criteria: using the text to justify claims about central ideas.

As this example illustrates, the teacher "stacked" challenges by presenting students with increasingly complex problems that invite them to productively engage with uncertainty while deepening and applying their knowledge of required academic concepts and skills.

Stop-Think-Do-Learn Connection

Lesson unplanning provides a great opportunity for you and your students to become familiar with the *stop-think-do-learn* action principles. You will have the opportunity to cycle through these principles when unplanning a lesson, and you can give students the same opportunity by inviting them to unplan some activities, too. They can also apply these principles when working on the beyond-classroom challenges described in Part 2 of this book. Figure 4.3 provides an overview of how the action principles connect with lesson unplanning.

FIGURE 4.3
The Stop-Think-Do-Learn Connection: Lesson Unplanning

	Stop	Lesson unplanning requires you to stop and explore your existing lessons, activities, and assignments to see how you might introduce more uncertainty into those learning experiences.
	Think	Replacing *predetermined* features with *to-be-determined* features as a means of introducing uncertainty requires you to generate multiple ideas and then select the most actionable possibilities.
	Do	You then have an opportunity to implement and test out these more complex learning experiences with your students.
	Learn	You can then reflect on this process and determine whether you need to make further modifications to provide students with a more appropriate range of challenges, from simple to complex.

 **Getting Started**

The following steps will help you and your students transform simple challenges into more complex ones and design new tasks that invite students to engage with uncertainty.

Start small and strive to go big.

What: A key benefit of lesson unplanning is that you can start by making slight adjustments to existing lessons. Transforming an already problematic activity or assignment into a more challenging one is a small risk. By continuing to make minor adjustments, you will develop your confidence and capacity to incorporate larger challenges into your curriculum.

How: A good way to get started is to select some learning tasks and experiences you already want to improve. Once you have transformed these into more complex tasks and successfully implemented them in your classroom, you can set some more ambitious goals. You might, for instance, invite students to unplan a simple challenge themselves. Doing so can help them learn first-hand how introducing more uncertainty makes a task more challenging and can encourage them to continually push themselves to take on even greater challenges. Encourage students to think about how a challenge can be extended in other ways, too, to help prepare them for beyond-classroom legacy challenges.

Be creative within constraints.

What: Creativity thrives within constraints (Beghetto, 2016c). Although many people recognize that creativity involves uncertainty, they may not realize that it also requires meeting task constraints. Indeed, creativity researchers tend to agree that creativity blends originality with meeting task constraints in a particular context (Amabile, 1996; Plucker, Beghetto, & Dow, 2004; Stein, 1953). Consider a student who responds to a double-column subtraction exercise on a math quiz (*Demonstrate you understand subtraction: What is 24 – 13?*) by writing a poem that uses a bonsai tree as a metaphor to suggest that beauty can be added through subtraction. This might be considered an *original* response, but it's not a creative one because it fails to meet the task constraint of solving the problem.

Lesson unplanning provides creative openings (i.e., to-be-determined features) in the predetermined constraints of your assignments and tasks. As a result, students have an opportunity to respond creatively by providing their own original responses to the challenge while working within the challenge's constraints.

How: You can support your students in responding creatively by making sure that they understand both the nonnegotiable constraints and the aspects that require their original response. Returning to the double-column subtraction example, you can challenge students to come up with as many different ways of solving a particular problem as they can while making sure they provide a mathematically accurate response. For example, a student asked to demonstrate all the ways she knows how to solve the subtraction problem 24 – 13 could show several methods beyond the standard borrowing strategy—for example, "First remove the 4 and 3, subtract 10 from 20, which equals 10, then subtract the 4 from the 10, which equals 6; finally, add 3 to the 6, which equals 9" (adapted from Kamii, 2000).

* *

Summing Up

In this chapter, we dived into the process of lesson unplanning, a dynamic process that allows you to breathe new life into seemingly dead-end lessons and transform simple challenges into more complex ones. The approach will also help you design new tasks that provide students with opportunities to productively engage with uncertainty. Given that this is a self-directed process and not an exact science, you have the freedom to decide which topics or lessons you want to unplan and the extent to which you want to unplan the activities in those topics.

By making lesson unplanning a regular and transparent practice in your classroom, you can help cultivate a spirit of possibility thinking and productive problem solving. As your students become more familiar with the process, they, too, can join in by removing features of tasks and assignments to make them more complex. You will still play a crucial role in ensuring that students are aware of and adhering to the "nonnegotiable" criteria.

Developing a working understanding of this process will also prepare you and your students for designing and implementing the complex beyond-classroom challenges described in Part 2 of this book. The chapters that follow introduce legacy challenges and explain how you and your students can use them to design solutions to problems that push learning beyond the walls of the classroom.

Part 2

Legacy Challenges:
Going Beyond the Classroom

5

Introducing Legacy Challenges

What if you could find a way to unleash your students' problem solving and creativity by pushing their learning beyond the walls of the classroom?

Complex classroom challenges provide students with opportunities to engage with uncertainty within the school limits for a finite time span. They provide a good warm-up for beyond-classroom challenges, which require students to put their academic learning to use beyond the walls of the classroom. In this chapter, we explore a type of beyond-classroom challenge called *legacy challenges*.

What Is a Legacy Challenge?

Legacy challenges are student-directed creative endeavors that aim to make a positive, lasting contribution. Students' overarching goal is to identify and develop a solution to an open-ended problem facing them, their school, their community, or the world beyond. Legacy challenges require students to address the following four questions (Beghetto, 2017a):

1. **What is the problem?** Students must start by identifying a problem that they view as meaningful. Legacy challenges are aimed at tackling issues or problems that are important to young people and may not be visible to adults.

2. **Why does it matter?** Students are responsible for providing a rationale for why the problem is important to them and others, including the greater community. This involves exploring the ethical and moral dimensions of a problem, asking themselves questions such as *Who will benefit*

55

from a solution to this problem? What if we don't address this problem? and *What are the potential costs or drawbacks of trying to address this problem?*

3. **What are we going to do about it?** To answer this question, students need to break down the problem and determine small steps they can take toward addressing it. Legacy challenges require students to identify "nimble solutions," or solutions that can be quickly tried out, refined, and tried again.

4. **What lasting contribution will we make?** The answer to this question is what makes a legacy challenge unique. It requires students to take a long view of the problem they are addressing, developing a solution that can be passed on from one cohort of students to the next or given to community partners to carry on. The sustainability of these solutions distinguishes legacy challenges from other problem-solving approaches.

Depending on the type of problem students identify, the solution might take the form of a procedure (e.g., a new school process for handling under-the-radar bullying), a social program (e.g., a training program to promote healthy teen relationships), a student-run business (e.g., a T-shirt company that raises awareness of social problems), or a computer program or app (e.g., a game elementary students can play to develop their confidence). For the sake of simplicity, the vehicle that students design and use to implement their solution can be referred to as a "legacy project" (Beghetto, 2017a).

A variety of learning approaches and experiences share certain features with legacy challenges, including service learning (Stanton, Giles, & Cruz, 1999), Eagle Scout and Girl Scout projects, enrichment activities (Renzulli, Gentry, & Reis, 2004), real-world projects (Boss, 2015), and design challenges (Brophy, Klein, Portsmore, & Rogers, 2008). Although some of the student work that results from these efforts might be classified as legacy projects, not all of it meets the criteria. Figure 5.1 provides a summary of the defining elements of legacy challenges.

You can use this list of defining elements not only to guide your own efforts in developing legacy challenges but also to introduce your students to legacy challenges. A starter exercise would be to have students use the list as a reference to help them identify or describe projects or learning experiences that meet these criteria.

Are Legacy Challenges Worth Your Time?

If one thing is true about teaching, it's that there is no such thing as extra time. Because legacy challenges do take time and effort, you'll need to find creative ways to carve out the space you need. Consider incorporating a weekly student "genius

---

FIGURE 5.1
Legacy Challenges Are . . .

For Students, By Students (FSXS)
Legacy challenges are designed by students, for students. *Students* identify a problem to be addressed, *students* develop the rationale for why the problem matters, *students* design an approach to address it, and *students* determine how the work will live on.

A Creative Response to Uncertainty
Legacy challenges help students learn how to respond productively to uncertainty in the form of addressing problems that matter to them, their schools, their communities, and beyond.

A Process and a Product
Developing a solution to a student-identified problem is a key feature of legacy challenges, but it is only half the story. Legacy challenges are also about learning from the process and sharing that learning with others. Students are expected to document their process, including the problems they initially identified, how those problems changed, and the solutions they developed and implemented, whether successful or not.

Problem Solving All the Way Through
From initial identification of a problem through implementation of a solution, you and your students will be continually engaged in problem solving. By identifying a problem and why it matters, students will have to figure out what they plan to do about it. Even after students have arrived at a solution, they will be faced with the challenges of making that solution work, determining what is or is not working, and ensuring that their project makes a lasting contribution.

Collaborative Endeavors
Legacy challenges require students to collaborate with external partners and experts to bring outside learning into the classroom, push learning beyond the walls of the classroom, and establish enduring relationships that help ensure the work will live on.

Exhibited and Curated
Legacy challenges require students to exhibit their ideas and work for critique and feedback. The "behind-the-scenes" stories and artifacts of the challenge are maintained and made accessible to anyone who is interested in learning from or replicating the work. This also means that learning, reflection, and revision can continue even after students' work has been exhibited and curated.

Never-Ending Projects
By definition, legacy projects never end. Thus, they should be designed in a way that ensures that the work carries on even after the challenge ends. Legacy projects are designed to be sustainable, maintainable, and, ultimately, passed on to new generations of students who can continue to ensure that the work makes a lasting contribution.

---

hour" or genius breaks (breaking the hour into three 20-minute segments throughout the week) into the class schedule (Juliani, 2014). Other options include incorporating time for legacy projects into homeroom meetings, student council meetings, an existing school club, or a new club designed specifically to work on legacy challenges.

Regardless of how you make time for legacy challenges, be sure you've asked yourself one important question: *Is it worth it?* You may have already asked yourself this question, and you can certainly count on students, colleagues, administrators, and students' parents to ask it.

Several arguments speak to the benefits of legacy challenges. Indeed, the core argument of this book maintains that complex challenges teach students how to respond productively to uncertainty, aligning with school's fundamental goal of preparing students for the unknowable future.

Many who have had the courage to embark on similar efforts have been amazed at the quality and impact of the resulting student work. As Larry Rosenstock, founder and CEO of the High Tech High network of project-based charter schools, explained in the documentary *Most Likely to Succeed*, once you see what students are capable of, "you have that feeling like we all have, like how did they do that!?" (Whiteley, 2015).

How Can I Prepare Students for Legacy Challenges?

Once you've helped students develop an understanding of what legacy challenges are, it's time to prepare them to tackle a legacy challenge themselves. I suggest starting by presenting students with models to learn from and then leading them through the five-step process of designing their own legacy project.

Presenting Models

A great way to begin is to provide models. You can invite accomplished professionals from various disciplines into the classroom, in person or virtually, to describe the kinds of open-ended challenges they have addressed in their professional work and walk students through the process they used to successfully address their challenges, including their productive struggle and any setbacks they experienced.

Another way is to show students previous examples of legacy projects so that they can learn from other students who have successfully solved complex challenges. Examining past legacy projects helps students learn about the behind-the-scenes process and develop an understanding of the *who, what, when, where, why,* and *how* of complex challenges (Root-Bernstein & Root-Bernstein, 2017). It's not difficult to find real-life accounts of young people who have developed successful projects to address complex challenges.

For example, after a group of 4th graders in Marin County, California, watched a National Geographic film and discussed endangered species, one student asked, "But what can we do?" The teacher, Laurette Rogers, reached out to a California State trainer from an adopt-a-species program who suggested a few possibilities; the students voted to help the endangered freshwater shrimp. After spending several months learning all they could about the shrimp and its habitat, they found that the problem stemmed from a watershed issue and started working to restore the habitat. Their project continued year after year and eventually grew into a network of teachers, students, parents, farmers, businesses, and other agencies working toward habitat restoration (Rogers, 1996; Stone & Barlow, 2010).

This project, which has a legacy of more than 20 years, has made a positive and lasting contribution to both the local environment and the young people involved. As Megan, a student from the original 4th grade class that designed and launched the project, explained, "I think this project changed everything I thought we could do . . . it did show me that kids can make a difference in the world, and that we are not just little dots" (Rogers, 1996, p. 31).

Resources abound where you can find examples of projects, some of which meet the criteria of legacy projects and some of which do not. Figure 5.2 provides a list of websites that you and your students can explore to find project examples and practice distinguishing legacy challenges from similar efforts.

There are a few guiding questions you can use to help students learn from these models (adapted from Root-Bernstein & Root-Bernstein, 2017):

- How was the problem or challenge initially identified?
- What process or approach was used to address the challenge?
- What kinds of struggles, setbacks, and barriers were experienced and overcome?
- How was the solution to the challenge received, supported, or rejected by the broader community?

Explaining the Steps

Once you've taken some time to explore models of successful legacy projects, you can lead students through the five-step process of developing, implementing, and learning from a legacy challenge:

Step 1. You pose the challenge. A legacy challenge starts with you introducing students to legacy challenges and inviting them to start thinking about a problem they would like to tackle.

Step 2. Students identify a problem and an approach for addressing it. Next, students work on identifying a problem and then generate, test out,

---

FIGURE 5.2
Finding Examples of Legacy Challenges

Note: Given that websites are continually updated, you may need to search for "projects" or "real-world projects" on these sites to identify examples.

- **Edutopia:** https://www.edutopia.org/project-based-learning
- **High Tech High:** https://www.hightechhigh.org/student-work/student-projects
- **Buck Institute for Education:** http://www.bie.org/project_search
- **White House Science Fair:** https://obamawhitehouse.archives.gov/node/326121
- **Google Science Fair:** https://www.googlesciencefair.com/en

and refine their potential solutions to that problem. This process includes establishing partnerships with members of the community and outside experts to develop a plan for implementing and sustaining the work.

Step 3. Students implement their solutions. Because legacy projects are focused on gradually working toward addressing problems, students come up with lean solutions until they can establish a feasible long-term solution. During this step, students may find they need to pivot and find a different solution or even a different problem to address. The path from challenge to sustainable solution is not always linear or predictable, but the gradual work leading up to a sustainable solution is designed to be doable.

Step 4. Students tell their story in a learning exhibition. Students participate in a learning exhibition to share their experiences with the problem-solving process, regardless of whether their efforts have been successfully launched. This keeps the focus on what students have learned from the *process* of engaging with uncertainty.

Step 5. Students' work is curated and sustained. You and your students find ways to curate the work (e.g., hosting it on a school website) and establish a plan to ensure that it makes a lasting contribution.

A legacy challenge includes various additional sub-steps along the way, but this five-step big picture will help you and your students conceptualize the major milestones. Subsequent chapters break down these steps and provide further details on how to address each one.

The Legacy Challenge Planning Canvas

Students need support and guidance in designing a legacy challenge, as they do with all complex challenges. A simple Legacy Challenge Planning Canvas (LCPC) can help structure this process. Based on the popular business canvas planning tool used by entrepreneurs and start-ups (Maurya, 2012), an LCPC is a one-page planning tool (see Figure 5.3; this form is also available for download at http://www.ascd.org/ASCD/pdf/books/Beghetto2018forms.pdf) that provides a quick way for you and your students to design and keep track of the core components of a legacy challenge.

The LCPC is an indispensable tool throughout each phase of the legacy project design and implementation process. High school educator Christine Bland has found that the LCPC enables her students to think through their ideas, provide feedback to one another, and focus on more substantial project ideas that can leave a lasting impact (personal communication, 2017). In addition to

FIGURE 5.3
Legacy Challenge Planning Canvas

What is the problem?	Why does it matter?	What are we going to do about it?
Stop Think Do Learn	Stop Think Do Learn	Stop Think Do Learn

What lasting contribution will we make?	Whom are we helping?	Who is helping us?
Stop Think Do Learn	Stop Think Do Learn	Stop Think Do Learn

What materials do we need?	How are we monitoring progress and impact?	
	Progress monitoring	*Impact monitoring*
Stop Think Do Learn	Stop Think Do Learn	Stop Think Do Learn

helping students plan projects in class, the LCPC can also provide potential part-ners and audiences with a succinct overview of all the aspects of a legacy project.

The planning canvas is made up of eight compartments, each of which includes a design question requiring students to use the *stop-think-do-learn* principles to answer the question and plan this feature of their legacy chal-lenge. Let's take a closer look at these design questions.

1. **What is the problem?** The first compartment requires students to spec-ify the problem they will address. As we've established, this should be a problem that students have identified as relevant to them, their school, their community, or the world beyond. This compartment is one of the most dynamic of the LCPC because the problem likely will change more than once and in many ways, from small to radical, over the course of a legacy challenge. Rarely does a problem stay the same from its conception through the implementation phase.

2. **Why does it matter?** Once students have identified a problem, they need to learn more about it. This includes obtaining feedback and perspectives from various stakeholders and developing their understanding of why it

is important and needs to be addressed. Students will also need to practice communicating the importance of their problem to others so that they can obtain support and assistance from external partners. As students spend time thinking about the importance of the problem and receiving feedback from others, they will likely refine their rationale. As a result, this compartment, too, will be updated and revised over time.

3. **What are we going to do about it?** Students use this compartment to describe a feasible and sustainable solution to the problem they have identified. During the planning phase, students will need to draw on their existing knowledge about the problem, identify areas where they need additional information, establish external partnerships, and determine some initial steps they can take toward addressing the challenge. Students will then test out their ideas and make necessary modifications along the way. Consequently, the potential solutions will be refined throughout the planning and implementation process.

4. **What lasting contribution will we make?** This compartment, which represents the fourth core component of a legacy challenge, requires students to explain how the work will be curated, sustained, and passed on from one cohort of students and partners to the next.

5. **Whom are we helping?** This compartment helps keep the beneficiaries of legacy challenges front and center. Doing so ensures that your students' work maintains a human face and reminds students and partners whose needs are being served by their effort. Although the beneficiaries may change over the course of the challenge as the initial target audience grows or shrinks, keeping a focus on whom students are helping with their project will focus and motivate their efforts as they get further into designing and implementing their solutions.

6. **Who is helping us?** This compartment of the LCPC requires students to outline whom they will be partnering with to help them tackle the challenge. Partners can include community organizations, outside experts, and any other individual or group that will be providing assistance, feedback, and support in developing, implementing, and sustaining the work.

7. **What materials do we need?** In this compartment, students list the resources they need to implement and sustain their solutions. Materials can include anything from digital planning and communication tools to material resources, such as building materials and financial resources.

8. **How are we monitoring progress and impact?** This compartment of the canvas prompts students to identify how they will monitor their progress toward implementing their solutions and whether those solutions are

having a positive and lasting impact. Students can assess the impact of their work on their target audience through such measures as satisfaction surveys, number of downloads, and number of views. They can also list anything you have planned to monitor impact on academic learning, such as weekly check-ins; Chapters 6 and 11 provide ideas and tools to help you and your students monitor and document academic learning in legacy projects.

When filling out the LCPC, students should respond to each question using a few clearly written and succinct sentences or even bullet points. The purpose of this document is not to provide exhaustive details but, rather, to provide enough information to give someone who knows nothing about the challenge a quick snapshot of the key details.

Because the LCPC is a living document that students continually update and revise, they can use it to track the changes they make to each compartment. You can help students find a simple way to keep track of changes, like having them label each update with a new version number. Starting with version 1.0 (v1.0), students can add .1 for each minor change (v1.1) and 1 for each more substantial change (v2.0). It may also be helpful to add a dating convention to keep track of when the versions changed (v1.1_month_day_year). Adding a dating convention comes in particularly handy when it's time for students to share the story of how their challenge took shape over time.

Finally, prior to using the LCPC with your students, you may find it helpful to draft some responses to the questions on the canvas yourself. You can do this in 15 minutes or so; just get some initial ideas down. Then request feedback from one of your colleagues, or, better yet, work with a colleague or two and draft a few potential examples. This exercise can help you become familiar with the key features of the planning canvas, which will help you better guide your students as they create their own. It will also give you a chance to recognize and anticipate how the *stop-think-do-learn* action principles apply to each compartment of the design canvas.

 Getting Started

The following steps will help you and your students get started understanding, designing, and implementing legacy challenges.

Establish some initial guidelines.

What: Just as with any other complex challenge, you will need to provide students embarking on a legacy challenge with clear expectations and the necessary structure. These guidelines include everything from the project's time frame to which academic skills students need to demonstrate in their projects.

How: When preparing to launch a legacy challenge, working through the following questions can help you clarify and establish some initial guidelines and expectations:

- How much total time will you devote to the legacy challenge? How often will you provide class (or other structured) time for students to work on these projects (e.g., every Friday)? How much time will you devote to each session (e.g., 20 minutes)?
- What specific skills do you want students to be able to demonstrate and document as they work on their projects? Do you have specific tools or technologies you want students to use when working on their projects? How will you have students document what they learn in their projects?
- Will this legacy project be connected to some other academic or after-school projects (e.g., research project, invention fair, after-school service learning club)?
- What are your expectations for students with respect to working alone or working in teams? How will you handle situations where students want to switch teams, join teams, combine teams, or work alone?
- How often will you check in with teams and individuals? How long will these check-ins take? What kinds of things will you expect during these check-ins?
- What date will you set for a public showcase of your students' learning? Where will the showcase occur? Who will be invited to the showcase?

It is OK if you are not sure how to answer all the above questions or if you have more questions to add to this basic list. The remaining chapters provide additional ideas and suggestions for how to plan for and establish guidelines and supports necessary for your students. Chapter 10, for instance, provides ideas for how you can set up the legacy challenge to require students to document academic learning. Doing so can help justify your use of class time for designing and implementing a legacy challenge. Just make sure academic content goals do not overtake the primary goal of solving the problem. (See Chapter 10 for a more detailed discussion of how to document academic learning in legacy projects.)

To eat an elephant, take small bites.

What: The prospect of tackling a legacy challenge may seem overwhelming, so manage the process by breaking down the challenge into smaller pieces.

Breaking larger problems into sub-problems is one way expert problem solvers approach complex challenges (Newell & Simon, 1972).

How: Plan sessions for working on legacy challenges that have only one or two agenda items to cover. If you don't complete all the items on the agenda in one session, you can roll them over to the next session. This will allow you to devote whatever amount of time you can to a set of agenda items. Whether you have only 15 or 20 minutes during homeroom one day a week or are able to allot more time spread over multiple days a week, the key is to consistently provide time for students to work through the agenda items.

The LCPC is a great tool to help organize and keep track of the key components of a legacy challenge. The chapters that follow share various ideas, activities, and tools to help you and your students break down the challenge into smaller parts—starting with identifying and refining a problem and continuing all the way to planning and implementing a solution.

Showcase learning when it is best for you and your students.

What: When introducing a legacy challenge to your students, be sure to let them know that they will be presenting the story of what they learned from the process to a public audience—regardless of whether they have implemented their solution. You and your students will need to determine who makes up the audience, but generally speaking it should include people beyond the classroom (e.g., other students, parents, members of the community, the general public). It is important to help students become comfortable with the fact that legacy challenges aren't clear-cut, and that the learning exhibition's purpose is to give students an opportunity to discuss the messiness of the work and what they have learned along the way. As such, the *product* of their efforts will serve as more of a backdrop to the *process*, which will take center stage.

Given that legacy challenges are "never-ending projects" designed to live on beyond the time you and your students devote to planning and implementation, the learning exhibition should come at a point after students have had time to develop and, ideally, implement their solution.

How: Tell your students that the learning exhibition is based on a "work in progress." The learning exhibition should come at a time that you have determined is best for your and your students' schedule (not based on when a challenge is "finished"). If, for instance, you are devoting six weeks to a legacy challenge, you might want to set the learning exhibition for the eighth or ninth week.

Alternatively, you may allot a few hours each week during the first half of the school year for planning and then a few hours each week during the second

half of the school year for implementation. In that case, you may want to schedule your learning exhibition on an evening during one of the final weeks of the
school year. Again, the date should be determined by your own circumstances
and schedule.

Finally, you may find it helpful to let students know that you will provide
them with frequent opportunities to discuss their ideas with multiple audiences
both in and out of the classroom. By the time they make their presentations at
the public learning exhibition, they will have had plenty of practice discussing
their ideas and what they have learned from their work.

Summing Up

Legacy challenges are complex, sometimes overwhelming enterprises. When
introducing your students to legacy challenges, it's important to provide them
with an adequate orientation. Although it might feel tempting to jump right in
after a brief preview, providing students with a thorough orientation will help
ensure that they are ready to embark on identifying and solving a complex,
meaningful challenge.

Students should come away from the orientation with a sense of possibility,
ready to engage with the uncertainty of problem finding. They should also recognize that despite the open-ended nature of the challenge, you will still be providing
instructional support and guidance along the way and breaking down the challenge into more manageable tasks and goals.

The chapters that follow introduce additional planning tools and activities that will help you guide students in designing their first legacy challenge.
Your next step is to help students get started on identifying a problem to
address. The following chapter provides insights, examples, and activities to
help you and your students take this important step of designing a legacy
challenge.

6

What Is the Problem?

What if you encouraged your students to identify a problem that matters to them and gave them enough support, guidance, and encouragement to solve it?

Once you have introduced students to legacy challenges, their next step is to address the question *What is the problem?* Given that the problem students identify is the driving force of a legacy challenge, it is important that they take sufficient time to find one that they really care about solving. This should be a problem that, once addressed, has the potential to make a positive and lasting impact on them, their school, their community, or the world beyond. To do so, students will need to engage in *problem finding*.

Problem Finding in Legacy Challenges

Problem finding, which simply refers to identifying and defining a problem, is one of the most important yet most easily overlooked aspects of high-quality legacy challenges. Problem finding is what differentiates complex challenges from more routine forms of problem solving (Kozbelt, Beghetto, & Runco, 2010; Mackworth, 1965), and investing time in this process is what distinguishes accomplished problem solvers from those who are less adept (Sawyer, 2012).

In the context of designing a legacy challenge, problem finding encompasses four steps:

1. Generating candidate problems;
2. Narrowing down the possibilities;
3. Reconsidering the remaining possibilities; and
4. Selecting an initial problem and a legacy team.

Generating Candidate Problems

The first step of problem finding is to generate as many candidate problems as possible. I suggest starting by asking students to individually come up with as many problems as they can that face them, their peers, the school, the community, or the world beyond. You can give students several options for listing their ideas. For example, they could simply write down their ideas as they arise and later label them by category (e.g., *school problems*, *community problems*, and *societal problems*), or they could first create a column for each of these categories and then brainstorm problems within each category.

Students who have little or no experience identifying problems to solve will understandably need some guidance. You can help "prime the pump" by providing a few examples of problems that you believe are relevant to students. The examples might represent issues that you and your colleagues have observed (e.g., students experiencing isolation in the lunch room or playground) or needs that you have identified in the broader community (e.g., a lack of community connections that could be addressed through a creative project such as a mural).

Consider Iowa BIG, an initiative-based program that matches high school students from four Iowa school districts with authentic community challenges. As part of the experience, Iowa BIG hosts a "Partner Palooza" where local businesses and organizations pitch real problems for students to solve, and students get to select from a pool of problems to address. Projects have included building an edible community landscape, designing and building an aquaponics system in a 20-foot shipping container, designing a remodel of a historic urban farm, and developing a web-based app to help communities coordinate volunteers during and after disasters (Iowa BIG, n.d.). You can use a similar model by inviting community businesses and organizations to pitch problems to students. This is one example of how challenges facing the community can become part of the curriculum (Boss, 2017).

Just make sure students don't view any examples or suggested projects as requirements. When highlighting example problems, stress that these are *not* problems that your students should or need to address, but simply the *kinds* of problems that they themselves might identify as relevant. This is particularly important if this is your students' first legacy challenge. Given the amount of time and effort that goes into a legacy challenge, students should pick passion projects that they care deeply about and want to stick with even when the going gets tough.

If you're concerned that providing examples might propel students to focus too narrowly on the specifics you are sharing, you may choose to highlight a few general themes (e.g., promoting nutrition, making a difference in the community, addressing a problem facing young people). The activity at the end of this chapter provides guidelines and prompts that you can use to guide students through this process.

Another way to get students' wheels turning is to encourage them to uncover hidden problems. Sometimes the most powerful results happen when students identify problems that no one else is aware of or sees as problems. Students should be open and creative, brainstorming novel ideas and taking as many different perspectives as possible when generating those ideas.

For example, say a community has a food pantry to support families in need, but the majority of food items provided have limited nutritional value. The hidden problem in this scenario would be that community members who live in poverty have inadequate access to affordable and healthful food options.

Another example of a hidden problem is under-the-radar bullying, which may happen daily without being noticed by adults or even most students. Such bullying may occur even in a school that has a well-established anti-bullying program and far fewer overt bullying incidents than the average school in the district.

Narrowing Down the Possibilities

Once students have generated as many problems as they can, have them take a moment to review their lists. Ask them to look for possible overlapping problems (e.g., students eating alone in the lunch room, student cliques, kids with no one to play with on the playground) and see whether they might combine them into one challenge (addressing the problem of social isolation). Once students have finalized their individual lists, assemble small teams of students to narrow down their lists.

One way to form these teams is by random assignment. You can simply ask students to number off 1 to 3 (or up to 5, depending on your class size and preferred team size) and then join with classmates with the same number to form their temporary problem-narrowing teams. Explain to students that these teams are not necessarily the teams they'll be working in for their legacy challenge, nor will they necessarily end up addressing the problems they discuss in these teams. Being clear about the goal of this step can relieve concerns students may have about being stuck with certain topics or teams and enable them to focus on the task at hand.

Once students are assigned to their problem-narrowing teams, ask them to take turns reading their individual *full lists* of problems while their teammates listen, ask clarifying questions, and keep track of commonly identified problems. Once everyone in the group has had an opportunity to share, teammates work together to identify the two problems that they collectively believe are the most important. Encourage students to spend as much time as necessary to think through all the problems and arrive at an agreed-upon top-two list. In the rare event that students cannot reach consensus, it is OK for them to nominate more than two problems.

Having students work together, rather than individually, to narrow down the problems ensures that all problems are properly considered and not prematurely eliminated, as might be the case if students independently reviewed their own lists.

A helpful strategy during this step is to create problem "mash-ups" that combine two seemingly unrelated problems. Begin by encouraging students to try consolidating problems, especially those that don't seem connected. This exercise can lead to some of the most interesting, innovative, and impactful legacy challenges. Creativity researchers (Rothenberg, 2014) have noted that many creative breakthroughs emerge from the combination of seemingly unrelated or even opposite concepts.

To illustrate the process, let's take two seemingly separate problems that students have identified: (1) social isolation of elderly community members and (2) young people's limited understanding of healthful eating options. By encouraging students to consider possible connections between these problems, you can help them find a way to combine them into a more interesting and powerful legacy project: *Develop an annual "healthy options" dinner event prepared and hosted by students and elderly members of the community.*

A problem mash-up activity that you can use with your students is provided at the end of the chapter.

Reconsidering the Remaining Possibilities

Once the teams have identified their top two problems, you can have each group nominate a spokesperson who will share out its shortlist with the whole class. All students can then collectively reconsider the remaining possibilities.

You or a student will record and display the top choices of all the groups. Given that students may use unique or unclear descriptions of the problems they have nominated, it is helpful to ask the spokesperson from each group to clarify any unclear descriptions.

A group of students may, for instance, nominate the problem of "low-key grilling." Although they may have a clear understanding of what this means, you and others in and beyond the classroom may not. By modeling how to ask for clarification ("I'm not sure what you mean by 'low-key grilling'; can you explain that to us?"), you can help the group more clearly articulate the problem ("Oh, OK—'low-key grilling' is what we call a kind of 'under-the-radar' bullying that happens every day, but that adults in the school usually do not notice").

Once the problems have been listed and clarified, you can facilitate a whole-class discussion aimed at further consolidating candidate problems by identifying potentially similar problems that might be combined.

Selecting an Initial Problem and a Legacy Team

During this final phase of the problem-finding process, students select the problem that most resonates with them and assemble into initial legacy teams. Students can pick a problem they or their problem-narrowing team nominated or one that captured their interest during the whole-group discussion. A good way of facilitating this process is to write each problem on a large sticky note and place those notes in different parts of the room. You can then have students indicate their preference with a "standing vote" (i.e., standing next to the problem they have selected).

Students will form tentative teams with classmates who selected the same problem. Ideally, these teams should include four to five students. Legacy challenges are ambitious endeavors and do not work well as independent projects. If there is a team with fewer than three students, you'll want to ask them to select another problem. This is a good time to remind students that they will have a chance to change groups or topics later. As the teams continue to refine their problems, it is possible that problems will change or merge with other ideas or even that groups will disband or merge with other groups. When it comes to the size of student teams, there is no magic number. With teams of more than five members, you'll want to ensure that everyone on the team is contributing. If they are, great. If not, you may want to remind them that everyone is expected to contribute and encourage any students who seem less engaged to consider coming up with a new project idea that they are more interested in working on.

Working through the four steps of the problem-finding process will enable you and your students to arrive at your goal in one or two class periods. At this point, your students will be ready to draft an initial problem statement in the *What is the problem?* compartment of their Legacy Challenge Planning Canvas.

A Note on Student Sharing

Students, like all of us, need to learn how to provide (and receive) feedback in a productive way. If students fear sharing their ideas, then the entire process will come to a grinding halt. Ground rules can be very helpful in teaching students how to interact with one another in a positive, supportive manner (Beghetto, 2016a; Littleton & Mercer, 2013). Figure 6.1 provides some sample ground rules that you can use or modify for use with the problem-finding activity on page 75 and any other activity that requires students to work together and share their ideas.

FIGURE 6.1
Group Sharing Ground Rules

- We agree to take this process seriously.
- We agree to work together to identify the most important problems we can in the amount of time we have.
- We agree to share and respectfully listen to all ideas, no matter how silly or unusual they may seem.
- We agree to take our time and not rush through this process.
- We agree to ask for clarification on anything that we don't understand.
- We agree to try to have fun with this process.

The Stop-Think-Do-Learn Connection

Given that a primary goal of legacy challenges is to give students practice using the *stop-think-do-learn* action principles to respond to uncertainty, you can help students by asking them to recognize when they are using the principles. As you may have noted in reading this chapter, the problem-finding process provides multiple opportunities to apply these principles; these connections are highlighted in Figure 6.2.

FIGURE 6.2
The Stop-Think-Do-Learn Connection: Problem Finding

	Stop	Students stop and take time to explore all the various kinds of problems facing them, their school, their community, and the world beyond.
	Think	Students generate as many different problems as they can (divergent thinking) and then narrow down their options (convergent thinking).
	Do	Students share and discuss the problems they have identified, give and receive feedback on these initial problems, and narrow down their choices.
	Learn	Students reflect on the process, examine how their views about the problems have changed, and decide which problem(s) they will pursue.

Getting Started

The following steps will help you and your students embark on the first step of a legacy challenge: finding a problem.

Slow down and take your time.

What: The problem-finding stage necessitates taking the time to identify a problem that is truly important to address. Many students have developed the habit, when given assignments, of quickly determining what they need to do and how they need to do it. Although such a strategy might serve them well when they're working through a clearly defined learning exercise, it can be counter-productive when identifying a problem for a legacy challenge.

How: You will want to devote at least one class period to the problem-finding process. During this time, encourage your students to slow down and focus on identifying a problem that really matters to them. This includes thinking deeply about and seeking out various perspectives on potential problems.

You can also reinforce the idea that it is OK and even expected for students to change their minds about what problem they want to address. During problem finding, their goal is to spend time exploring problems until they land on one that is sufficiently complex and personally important. By encouraging students to stop and take the time they need to think about possibilities before moving forward, you can help ensure that they identify a problem they care enough about to stick with until it's solved.

Expect the unexpected.

What: There is always an element of the unknown in the problem-finding process. You may find yourself surprised by or uncomfortable with some of the topics that students identify. Some ideas are clearly out of bounds—for example, any that may cause harm or are driven by self-serving motives ("We want to make money for ourselves by finding items sold by the school store for less money on Amazon and then selling them at our own after-school bargain store"). At the same time, you do not want to be too quick to discourage ideas, particularly if those ideas have potential merit and students are passionate about the issue.

How: Instead of stifling potentially viable ideas by preemptively shutting down certain topics (Beghetto, 2013), prepare yourself and your students for handling out-of-bounds legacy challenge ideas. One of the best ways is to establish and discuss some general guidelines for legacy challenges, such as "Projects should focus on helping others rather than on benefiting the people working on the project," "Projects should make a positive impact and avoid causing harm," or "When coming up with ideas, think about both the intended and the potential unintended consequences of solving the problem." You can also tell students that you'll let them know when a topic seems self-serving or potentially harmful to others ("Remember that a key goal of a legacy challenge is to make a positive and lasting contribution").

In some cases, students may propose problems that address sensitive or polarizing topics, which may raise questions or concerns in the school or community. Again, you and your students can anticipate this by developing a student-endorsed process for vetting potentially sensitive topics. In this way, it will not come as a surprise to students when you let them know that you need to seek external feedback and approval on the topic: "I can see this is an important topic to you. As we discussed, some topics that take on sensitive issues may raise questions or concerns among members of our school and community. Let me check in with some of my colleagues and the principal and see whether we can find a way to explore this problem or some version of it."

By establishing general guidelines *with* your students, you can prepare yourself and them for deciding whether a particular topic is suitable for a legacy challenge. Innovative and successful problem solvers know how to read an environment and determine whether it is worth the risk to move forward with an idea. You can help students develop this aspect of creative metacognition (Kaufman & Beghetto, 2013) so that even when a problem gets denied, the process serves as a positive experience that builds students' understanding of which topics are appropriate for legacy challenges.

A Problem-Finding Activity

The activity outlined in Figure 6.3 can be used to facilitate a problem-finding session with your students. You can use the steps highlighted in this activity as is or modify them for your class (e.g., by simplifying the wording for younger students).

FIGURE 6.3
Activity: What Is the Problem?

Stop-Think-Do-Learn: Take time to consider what problems are important (*stop*); think about all the different problems affecting you and others and select the ones you think are most important (*think*); share out your ideas with others (*do*); reflect on this process and select a problem and an initial team to work with to address the problem (*learn*).

Teacher-Given Prompt

- *Purpose:* The purpose of this activity is to help you identify an initial problem for your legacy challenge and choose an initial legacy team.
- Before we start, let's review some ground rules [see Figure 6.1].
- Think of some different problems at school, at home, in our community, or beyond. Think about problems that you believe are important, that you want to help solve, and that, if solved, would make a positive difference in people's lives. Think about problems that other people may not have noticed or thought much about. Take 5–10 minutes and write down as many of these problems as you can.

Small-Group Share

- In small groups (three to five people), take turns sharing your lists. Notice any common problems as well as any unique ones.
- Try to come to an agreement on the two problems that your group believes are the most interesting and important. These can be a combination of similar problems. If there is a problem that you feel is very important but others in the group do not, you can keep that one, too. Write down your top choices.

Whole-Class Share

- Nominate a spokesperson to share out your top choices. As each group shares out its top choices, they are recorded and displayed for the whole class.

Teacher-Given Prompt

- As a class, we are now going to look at all these problems and see if we can combine any similar ones. When we're done, I will put the final options on sticky notes around the room.
- Now I want you to select only one of the problems by standing next to the appropriate sticky note. It can be a problem you came up with or a different one that has caught your interest.
- At this point, you will form a small group with your classmates who have selected the same problem. Groups should include three (minimum) to five (maximum) people. If you do not have enough people to form a group of three, you'll need to find another group. You'll have a chance to change groups or topics later, if you choose.

Summing Up

Ultimately, your role during the problem-finding stage of a legacy challenge is to spark possibility thinking in students as they generate, analyze, and narrow down possibilities. This phase is one of the most important parts of the planning process because the problem students identify is the driving force of their legacy challenge. It can also be one of the most intimidating aspects for students, particularly those who have never identified their own problems to solve. Be sure to give them plenty of time and encouragement as they engage in this process.

Your students should come away from their problem-finding session (or sessions) with an initial problem that they are interested in addressing and team members they are ready to work with. Make sure students recognize how they are applying the *stop-think-do-learn* principles and to document any changes to their problem statement on their LCPC, which they can keep in a physical or digital folder. They may also want to keep track of the initial lists of problems that they generated and the problem that their team has decided to pursue at this point in the process.

The next phase of the legacy project is problem refining. During this stage, some specifics of the initial problem—or even the entire problem—likely will change. It's important to let students know that their problem will probably be modified in the next phase of the process. Explain that they should not feel discouraged by the fact that they haven't "finished" this part of the canvas but instead recognize that their problem will continue to evolve over time. Working through the various stages of a legacy challenge is less about checking tasks off a list than about getting things ready to test out, revisit, and modify. Legacy challenges are as much about experiencing and learning from the process as they are about arriving at a solution.

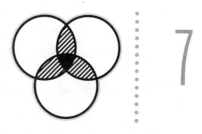

Problem Refining

What if you could provide opportunities for your students to experience the power of continually revisiting and revising their thinking?

Once students have identified a potential problem, they may feel tempted to move directly into generating solutions. That would be a mistake. At this stage, it's important for students to take the time to further clarify and refine their problem to ensure that they understand its key features—including whether the problem actually *is* the problem, as opposed to a symptom of a deeper issue. Problem refinement helps students examine and make any necessary modifications to the problem they have selected. Once students have gone through the problem-refining stage, they will be ready to respond to two questions on their LCPC: *What is the problem?* and *Whom are we helping?*

Problem Refining in Legacy Challenges

In the context of designing a legacy challenge, there are four steps of problem refining:

1. Clarifying what is already known about the problem;
2. Thinking about the problem in new ways;
3. Drafting an audience impact statement; and
4. Making necessary revisions to the problem statement on the LCPC.

You can expect to spend two or three class periods on problem refining. In some cases, students may be able to complete this process in one class period; in other cases, students may need additional time. Providing ample time to engage in this process will help students recognize that focusing their problem is important work that takes time and effort.

Clarifying What Is Already Known About the Problem

The first step of problem refining is to help legacy team members clarify what they already know about the problem. One of the best ways of doing this is to have the team spend some time working through an initial clarification activity, like the one presented at the end of this chapter (Figure 7.4). This involves working through such questions as

- What kind of problem is this?
- Whom does this problem affect? (Who is the target audience? Who sees this as a problem?)
- What do you already know about the problem? (What experiences do you have with the problem? How did you become familiar with the problem?)
- Is there anything you are still unclear about when thinking about this problem?

Having teams go through this process serves three purposes. First, it gives students a chance to systematically identify what they already know about the problem and which aspects of the problem remain unclear. Second, it helps students develop the habit of making their thinking visible to others and seeking feedback on that thinking. Finally, clarifying what they know and don't know about the problem prepares students for a deeper exploration of their assumptions about the problem.

Thinking About the Problem in New Ways

This step of problem refining prompts students to rethink their assumptions about the problem by seeking feedback and alternative perspectives. This can be a particularly powerful process when students believe they already have a deep understanding of the problem. Regardless of students' level of familiarity with the problem they have identified, this phase of the work can uncover hidden aspects of the problem and point to areas in need of revision.

When you provide students with opportunities to question their assumptions, they "experience the power of the process" and see how doing so can bring out new ideas and perspectives (Chaudron, 2014). A simple yet powerful question you can pose to get students started in challenging their assumptions is, "What if the problem is the solution?" Recall Trisha Prabhu (p. 30), the teenager who flipped the assumption that technology is a cause of cyberbullying by viewing it, instead, as a potential solution. Questioning this common assumption led her to develop her ReThink app, which warns teens prior to posting potentially hurtful messages on social media.

Conversely, you may ask, "What if the solution is the problem?" Consider Anushka Naiknaware, who, as a middle school student, learned that the typical treatment for the chronic wounds that millions of people suffer from was to change the bandage every 12 hours, regardless of the nature of the wound (Sabatier, 2016). Anushka recognized that this solution was actually the problem: not all wounds are the same, and some need more frequent bandage replacement to help prevent infections and speed up the healing process. She took on this problem and developed a new solution: bandages with sensors that could detect moisture and indicate when the bandage needed to be changed.

Figure 7.1 lists some assumption flips tailored specifically for use with legacy challenges that you can use to help students question their assumptions about their problems. These assumption flips can be used to gain insight into a variety of complex challenges and problems (see Beghetto, 2016a; Weick, 1979). Assumption flipping is an enjoyable activity, often filled with surprising insights. It is also a powerful way to generate new possibilities for thinking about a problem and even point to possible solutions.

FIGURE 7.1
Assumption Flips

What if . . .

- The solution is the problem? | The problem is the solution?
- What seems to be working is broken? | What seems to be broken is working?
- An individual issue is a group issue? | A group issue is an individual issue?
- The cause is the effect? | The effect is the cause?
- Big problems are smaller than they seem? | Small problems are actually big ones?
- Something unique is common? | Something common is unique?
- What seems stable is fluid? | What seems fluid is stable?
- What seems good is bad? | What seems bad is good?
- What seems organized is chaotic? | What seems chaotic is organized?
- Things that seem similar are different? | Things that seem different are similar?
- Something needs to be added? | Something needs to be taken away?
- Old is new? | New is old?
- Future is past? | Past is future?
- What seems slow is fast? | What seems fast takes a long time?
- Things that seem to go together are separate? | Things that seem separate go together?
- Success is failure? | Failure is success?

A good way to help students practice using assumption flips is to engage in the exercise as a whole class. You can simply have a representative from each team describe the team's problem and whom it affects and then ask the rest of the class to use assumption flips to help the presenting team think about its problem in a new way. The nice thing about the assumption flips listed in Figure 7.1 is that they start with the question stem "What if?," which helps students realize that it is just a possibility to consider, not a pointed critique.

The activity at the end of this chapter (Figure 7.4) shows how you can use assumption flips to help students see their candidate problems in a new way. Assumption flips can also help students start identifying potential solutions to their problem. Having students engage in this type of exercise not only benefits the presenting team but also helps clarify and strengthen the ideas of the students providing the feedback (Gibson & Mumford, 2013).

Making Necessary Revisions

Using an assumption flip activity with your students will likely generate numerous ways of rethinking their problems. The benefit of this is that students will have many options to choose from when making revisions. The downside, of course, is that too many options can feel overwhelming (Ryan & Deci, 2006). It is therefore important to encourage students to base their revisions on what they believe makes the most sense for them as a group. In some cases, students will realize that the problem they initially identified is actually a symptom of a different or larger issue. Once students start digging into a problem, it is not uncommon for them to recognize that they are tackling a bigger problem than they had initially imagined. In such cases, students need to be ready to shift their focus to some specific aspect of the problem. Promoting healthier eating habits, for instance, is a much larger problem than it may initially seem to students. Students who choose this problem will quickly realize that unhealthy eating habits involve many different contextual, situational, social, and individual factors. They would do better to focus on one aspect of unhealthy eating habits, such as snack choices during school.

In other cases, students may choose to abandon their initial conceptualization of the problem and pursue a completely different challenge. Consider, for instance, a group of students who served on their high school's student government and wanted to reinvigorate school spirit and student engagement (Brasof, 2015). They came to realize that the problem was not a lack of school spirit but a deeper issue:

It wasn't that students didn't care about school and therefore didn't engage in classroom and school-wide activities, rather a rift in the school's instructional vision resulted in changes to the very aspects of school that many students enjoyed. . . . [S]tudents were not consulted about the structural and curricular adjustments, although [they were] most affected by the changes. (Brasof, 2015, pp. 1–2)

Make sure you and your class are aware of these possibilities so that students recognize they have "permission" to change their problem or topic. Your students may never have been given so much agency in making decisions about the problems they are working on, so reassure them that it is OK to rethink, modify, or entirely change their focus. This "focusing work" will continue throughout the process, even after students have started working on potential solutions to the problem.

There is, of course, something to be said for staying the course. In cases where students are having trouble making up their minds, it can be helpful and reassuring for you to ask them to stick with their current problem for now and change their direction later on, if they can provide a compelling reason to do so.

As always, remind students to keep track of the changes they have made by maintaining older versions of their work and using a simple labeling convention that tracks the versions of their statements and when those versions changed (e.g., v1.1_month_day_year).

The Stop-Think-Do-Learn Connection

Just as with the problem-finding stage, I recommend encouraging students to practice identifying when they are using specific action principles during the problem-refining process. You can also highlight how and when they are applying these principles. Figure 7.2 provides an overview of how the action principles connect with this stage of a legacy challenge.

	FIGURE 7.2 **The Stop-Think-Do-Learn Connection: Problem Refining**	
	Stop	Students stop and explore what they know and don't know about their problem and whom their problem affects.
	Think	Students generate different ways of looking at their problem by uncovering and flipping their assumptions and narrowing their focus to specific aspects of the problem.
	Do	Groups test out their ideas about the problems they have identified by sharing them and inviting feedback.
	Learn	Students reflect on this process, including how their views about the problem and whom it affects have changed, and revise their problem statements accordingly.

● ●

Getting Started

The following steps will help you and your students clarify, refine, and revise problems chosen for a legacy challenge.

Focus and dig deep.

What: Successful problem solvers realize that even when they feel like they have a good grasp on a problem, there is often much more to learn (Robertson, 2017). Deeper features of a problem emerge only after thorough exploration. Therefore, students' primary goal with problem refining is to clarify and focus their problems. This may involve homing in on some specific aspect of a problem or identifying an underlying issue that the team was not aware of before going through the problem-refining process.

How: You can help your students develop the habit of digging deep into the legacy problems they have selected. This starts with having them explore what they know about the problem and which aspects remain unclear.

You can also help your students understand that one key to successful problem solving—especially complex and open-ended problems—is to recognize that there is a lot more to problem refining than simply having identified a problem that everyone in the group agrees is important and worth addressing.

Your students will need to move beyond what they know (and don't know) by researching the problem using sources available beyond the classroom, including, if necessary, contacting experts and more knowledgeable people in their community or state, or beyond. Using tools like Google Hangouts and Skype, students can arrange meetings with leading experts on topics. If time zone is an issue, students can send questions via e-mail and ask experts to respond with a written or video message. Students can even create a "living" shared document (using a tool like Google Docs) where they keep a repository of growing information about their problems.

You can use the activity in Figure 7.4 to help your students view their problems from different perspectives and start digging deeper into the problems they have identified.

Help students extend their focus beyond the self.

What: Although legacy challenges invite students to identify problems that they think are important, the ultimate goal is to implement a solution that helps others. Some problems affect many different people in various ways. Students will likely need to narrow their focus to a primary target audience. This will help them further clarify the nature of their problem and prepare them to explore ways to address it.

How: You can help your students extend the focus of their problem beyond themselves by asking them to continually keep the target audience in mind. Doing so will add a human face to their work that, in turn, will help them make decisions about the problem in relation to their primary audience.

It is also important to let students know that the work they are doing is not a solitary endeavor. Even when working alone, they should be trying to clarify their thinking so that others can understand it. Legacy challenges require students to share their ideas with others, seek out multiple perspectives, and draw on those perspectives to view their problem in new ways.

The activity in Figure 7.4 can help students clarify whom their project will help, and the following chapter provides insights, ideas, and activities that you can use to help students further clarify why solving the problem matters and what positive contribution their work will make.

Know when to pivot and when to stay the course.

What: There will likely be several instances in the planning and implementation of a legacy challenge when students need to shift gears and go in a different direction. Pivoting, according to Ries (2011), refers to changing directions while keeping one foot planted on the ground. This means being ready to make a change when it is reasonable to do so. Consequently, it will be helpful for students to get used to the idea of pivoting and feel supported in doing so.

The flipside of knowing when to pivot is knowing when to stay the course. Whereas some of your students may resist pivoting when necessary, other students may give up on problems prematurely. Shifting gears or abandoning a challenge too soon or too frequently can quickly undermine students' efforts and result in a negative and demoralizing experience. Solving complex challenges requires knowing when to pivot and when to stay the course.

How: You can help students get used to pivoting by letting them know that it is OK—expected, even—to feel as though they need to change direction. Some students will still feel uncomfortable making this change and need to be reminded that they have your "permission" to do so. I recommend asking students simply to check in with you whenever they feel like a change is needed. You can give them your perspective and, ideally, leave the decision of whether to pivot up to them.

In addition to letting students know that they will likely pivot several times during the course of their legacy challenges, tell them that it is important to stay the course unless there is a compelling reason to change direction. Such a reason would stem from testing ideas (e.g., sharing and obtaining feedback from members of the community, experts, and other relevant sources)—not from fears or unsubstantiated beliefs that something may not work. Again, you and your students can establish a general guideline that they need to check in with you prior to changing direction. That way, you can help them decide whether to stay the course a bit longer or shift gears.

When deciding whether to keep a project going or to pull the plug, a critical thing to keep in mind, according to Laura McBain—K12 Lab Director of Community and Implementation for Stanford's design school—is "It's not your project, it's the kids' project" (personal communication, 2017). Sometimes you need to let them run with it and see if they can transform their interest into momentum. If, however, students start losing interest or dread working on it, it may be time to encourage them to move on to something else.

The activities in the remainder of this book provide various ways for students to test out ideas to obtain information that will help them decide whether to stay the course or change direction.

A Problem-Refining Activity

The purpose of this activity is to help teams further clarify their problem, practice flipping assumptions about their problem, and make any necessary revisions. In preparation for this activity, team members need to spend some time clarifying with one another what they already know about the problem. They will then nominate a spokesperson who can, in no more than two minutes, describe the problem, explain why it is a problem, and share whom it affects. The prompts and questions in Figure 7.3 can help groups get ready for the activity in Figure 7.4.

FIGURE 7.3
Pre-Activity Warm-Up Questions

Working together, see if you can come to some agreement about how to describe the problem, why it is a problem, and whom it affects.
- What kind of problem is this? Is it a common or an unusual problem? Do a lot of people know about this problem?
- Whom does this problem affect? Be as specific as possible. List as many different audiences and groups that might be affected by this problem as you can and circle the audience or group that you believe is most directly affected by the problem.
- Who is your primary audience?
- What do you already know about this problem? Have you or has anyone you know ever experienced this problem or issue?
  - Briefly describe everything you know about this problem, including whether you have experienced it.
  - How often have you experienced it?
  - Besides you, who are some people who might know about this problem (list as many people as possible)?
    - Pick one of those people.
    - What do you think this person would say about this problem?

Nominate a spokesperson from your team to share your problem.

FIGURE 7.4
Activity: Refining the Problem

Stop-Think-Do-Learn: Take your time to stop and listen to your peers' feedback (*stop*); think about all the different ideas you hear and select those that might focus your team's problem (*think*); share out ideas to receive feedback and provide feedback to other teams (*do*); make any necessary revisions to your problem statement on your LCPC (*learn*).

Teacher-Given Prompt

- We are going to take turns presenting our problems in teams, and we will help each team flip its assumptions about the problem so team members can refine it.

- Let's revisit our ground rules [see Figure 6.1].

- When each team presents, listen for anything that is unclear. If we're unclear on something, we will ask clarifying questions before flipping assumptions.

Presenting Team

- Briefly describe your problem, taking no more than one or two minutes: What is the problem? Why is it a problem? Whom does this problem affect?

Questions and Flips from Listening Teams

Listening teams: If there is anything unclear about how the presenter described the problem, ask the presenter to clarify.

Listening teams and teacher:
- Use assumption flips [see Figure 7.1 or come up with your own] to challenge assumptions about any part of the problem.
  - Remember that an assumption starts with "What if . . . ?"
- Each person in the listening teams is expected to provide at least one assumption flip.
- You and your students can provide multiple assumption flips as soon as everyone has had a chance to provide one flip.

Presenting team:
- Listen carefully to the assumption flips in relation to your problem.
- It may be helpful to jot down a few notes to keep them in mind.
- You are not allowed to speak during this time.

Presenting Team

- The presenter briefly discusses what was most helpful from the feedback, such as what helped you think about the problem in a new way or see it from a different perspective.

- The presenting team will make any necessary revisions to its statements in the *What is the problem?* and *Whom are we helping?* compartments of the LCPC.

- The presenting team will keep track of different versions of the problem by labeling each with its own version number and date of revision (e.g., v1.1_month_day_year).

· ·

Summing Up

Problem refining asks students to take a deeper dive into their problem and clarify what they already know about it, explore what makes this problem a problem, and identify aspects of the problem that remain unclear. This stage requires you and your students to adopt a loopback mindset, so that students learn that complex problem solving involves a persistent willingness to revisit a problem multiple times and in multiple ways. This includes challenging assumptions about the problem to gain new insights into the nature of the problem and even into how the problem might be addressed.

Once students have gone through the problem-refining stage, they will be able to establish clear statements in response to two questions in their LCPCs: *What is the problem?* and *Whom are we helping?*

In addition to further focusing and clarifying the problem, problem-refining sessions prepare students to establish a rationale for why the problem matters. As the next chapter discusses, addressing this question involves further examining what makes the problem a problem, considering the effect the problem has on other people, and understanding the consequences of not addressing the problem.

Why Does the Problem Matter?

What if you could help your students develop a strong rationale for the problem they have chosen and effectively communicate that rationale to an external audience to recruit support and potential partnerships?

Once students have refined their problem, it's time to establish their rationale for why the problem matters. Having a clearly identified problem and a strong rationale for addressing the problem puts students in a better position to establish external partnerships and explore ways to address the problem. Having a clear sense of the importance of the problem can also motivate them to sustain their effort when they face setbacks. One of the best ways to clearly communicate the importance of the problem is to draft a *value statement*.

Creating a Value Statement in Legacy Challenges

In the context of a legacy challenge, a value statement succinctly and persuasively encapsulates why the problem matters and why addressing it is worth students' and external partners' time and effort. A value statement is what students write in the *Why does it matter?* compartment of the LCPC. You can help students draft a value statement by giving them the following prompts:

1. Why is this a problem?
2. What will happen if nothing is done?
3. Why is solving the problem worth the effort?

You will want to devote at least one class period to having students draft a value statement. Providing ample time for students to clarify why their problem matters will go a long way toward helping them communicate the importance of their problem to others as well as sustain their motivation during difficult or tedious aspects of their project.

Why Is This a Problem?

To communicate the importance of addressing their problem, students first need to be able to explain why their problem is, in fact, a problem. The following sub-questions can help students clarify this: *What negative effect does this problem have on people? Who thinks it is a problem? Why should anyone (beyond those affected) care about this problem? How does it affect daily life?*

As an example, let's say a group of your students wants to address the problem of under-the-radar bullying (i.e., bullying that kids experience but adults don't see). It is something they know is happening, even though the principal has announced at schoolwide assemblies that reported instances of bullying have decreased dramatically. The students work through the sub-questions to clarify why the issue selected is a problem:

- *What negative effect does this problem have on people?* The bullying is causing a lot of stress for students. Some students no longer want to come to school; others have stopped attending certain after-school clubs. Students also worry that adults won't believe them or will think they are being "too sensitive" or "dramatic" when they raise their concerns about this type of bullying.
- *Who thinks it is a problem?* Students who are experiencing this type of bullying and those who are aware that it is happening.
- *Why should anyone (beyond those affected) care about this problem?* Under-the-radar bullying makes school a less welcoming place and has caused fear and anxiety for students. The problem also affects students who have not directly experienced it but who worry that they will become a target if they say something or try to stop it.
- *How does it affect daily life?* It is causing a lot of unnecessary stress and anxiety in students' daily lives in and out of school. Even on weekends and breaks, students think about it and feel some dread about returning to school.

Once students have worked through these questions, they can draft a response to the first part of the problem statement:

Why is this a problem? We have been told that reports of bullying have been declining since the beginning of the year and even gone to zero in the last month. Yet our peers have told us that the under-the-radar bullying they experience has gotten worse and more frequent. Even though adults don't seem to recognize it as a problem because kids have stopped reporting it, bullying is still a problem.

Addressing this aspect of the value statement helps students clarify why they have decided to focus on this problem as well as persuade others to support the planning, implementation, and sustained work of the legacy challenge.

What Will Happen If Nothing Is Done?

This question is closely related to *Why is this a problem?* but goes further, highlighting the potential long-term impact of leaving the problem unaddressed. To address this question, students will need to forecast the future impact of the problem, including whether its negative aspects will worsen over time, stay the same, or even get better. It is important that students not simply assume that a problem will get bigger over time; they need to present a reasoned argument for why it may get worse or stay the same. To be able to make such a prediction, students will need to conduct further research on the problem and think through any conditions that may contribute to these various possible outcomes.

Let's return to the hypothetical example of under-the-radar bullying. Realizing that students need to get a more concrete sense of the problem's prevalence, you encourage them to conduct a brief anonymous survey using Google Forms. They first work with the assistant principal to follow school guidelines and seek proper permission. Once they obtain permission, the students launch a brief survey during the first 10 minutes of every homeroom. Then, drawing from the results, they write the second part of their value statement:

> *What will happen if nothing is done?* We conducted an anonymous survey in every homeroom, which 80 percent of the student body responded to. Twenty-two percent of students who responded said they are experiencing bullying, and 68 percent said they believe that bullying has gotten worse since the beginning of the school year. We therefore think it is important to address this problem because if we do nothing about it, then we believe it will continue to get worse, at least from the perspective of those who are victims of this type of bullying.

As this example illustrates, your students will need to collect additional information to get a more concrete sense of the issue—how prevalent it is, whether it has gotten worse, and if there is anything they might be missing. They may also need to seek assistance from external partners who can provide insights into the growth, current state, and potential future state of this problem. In some cases, the problem may be so unusual or new that little is known about its genesis or the factors leading to its development. Even in such cases, students should do some preliminary work to find out as much as they can about the problem and what might happen if they leave the problem unaddressed.

One way you can facilitate this process is to have teams clarify what they already believe will happen if the problem isn't addressed. More specifically, you can ask each team member to take a few minutes to make a prediction as to whether the problem will stay the same, get better, or get worse. Regardless of students' choices, they will need to explain the reasoning behind their predictions. To help them with this prediction, have them consider what is already happening with the problem and imagine what would happen if everything stayed the same. How might this affect the people experiencing the problem? How might it affect others? What other effects might it have?

You can then have students list as many sources of information as they can think of that might help them make a more accurate prediction. These sources might include those found through Internet research, experts in the topic, and people who are currently experiencing the problem.

Finally, working in their project teams, students can share their perspectives and try to reach an agreement on their prediction, their rationale for that prediction, and sources to help them test out, refine, and revise their prediction. You can also have teams share their perspectives with the whole class to hear how other groups are thinking through their problems and to get feedback on their predictions and additional information sources.

Why Is Solving the Problem Worth the Effort?

The third and final question prompts students to establish an argument for why solving the problem is worth the effort. Being able to answer this question comes in handy when students experience the less exciting aspects of trying to solve a complex challenge. Having already thought about why it is worth the effort can help sustain students' effort when they face setbacks and other difficulties (Wigfield & Eccles, 2000).

The ability to communicate why solving the problem is worth the effort is also important when students are trying to establish external partners. Students will need to be able to succinctly explain why they are willing to put time and effort into solving the problem and why it is worth the time, effort, and resources of the external partner to help them address the problem.

Let's return one last time to the under-the-radar bullying problem. Having worked through the first two questions of the value statement, students are now ready to address the last question: *Why is it worth the effort?* Once they do so, students will have a draft of their value statement that they can include in the *Why does it matter?* compartment of their LCPC. They will then be ready to share it with potential partners, school administrators, community members, and anyone else who may endorse and support their next steps. The full value statement for the under-the-radar bullying problem follows:

Our Value Statement

[*Why is it a problem?*] We have been told that reports of bullying have been declining since the beginning of the year and even gone to zero in the last month. Yet our peers have told us that the under-the-radar bullying they experience has gotten worse and more frequent. Even though adults don't seem to recognize it as a problem because kids have stopped reporting it, bullying is still a problem.

[*What will happen if nothing is done?*] We conducted an anonymous survey in every homeroom, which 80 percent of the student body responded to. Twenty-two percent of students who responded said they are experiencing bullying, and 68 percent said they believe that bullying has gotten worse since the beginning of the school year. We therefore think it is important to address this problem because if we do nothing about it, then we believe it will continue to get worse, at least from the perspective of those who are victims of this type of bullying.

[*Why is it worth the effort?*] Finding a solution will be worth the effort because it will help make the daily lives of many of our peers better both in and out of school.

The Stop-Think-Do-Learn Connection

As with every stage of a legacy challenge, it's a good idea to have students practice identifying when they are using specific action principles as they work toward establishing a value statement. Figure 8.1 highlights how the action principles connect with this step.

FIGURE 8.1
The Stop-Think-Do-Learn Connection: Establishing a Value Statement

	Stop	Students stop and carefully explore why their problem is a problem, what will happen if nothing is done, and why it is worth the effort to solve it.
	Think	Students generate several ideas, consider and evaluate multiple perspectives, and narrow their focus to establish a clear and persuasive rationale for why their problem matters.
	Do	Students have numerous opportunities to share and test out their rationale. They give and receive feedback on their value statement.
	Learn	Students reflect on this process, including how their views about the importance of the problem have changed, and revise their value statements in the LCPC accordingly.

 Getting Started

The following steps will enable you to help students develop a strong rationale for their chosen problem and draft a persuasive value statement.

Take the necessary steps to go from empty guessing to informed prediction.

What: Establishing an argument for why a problem matters involves forecasting what might happen if the problem is not addressed. Although students cannot see into the future, their efforts to predict the potential outcomes should not be blind guesses. Rather, students should take the time they need to obtain information that will enable them to make a reasoned prediction.

How: One way to help students accomplish this task is to ask them to identify how, if at all, the problem has changed over time. They can seek out the perspectives of people who are experiencing the problem or have insight into the problem—for example, by conducting brief surveys or interviews—and ask them whether the problem has gotten better, stayed the same, or gotten worse over time. This may also require conducting research to find out what is known about the problem in the published literature. Students can also ask various people who are experiencing or otherwise know about the problem to share their perspectives on what they think will happen if the problem is not addressed. Once students have collected this information, they can write a statement forecasting what they think might happen if the problem is not addressed. They will also need to briefly describe their sources.

Encourage your students to obtain as many different perspectives as possible and deliver a nuanced claim, making clear when others do not agree with their prediction and providing the reason for why they nonetheless maintain their perspective.

Cultivate clear and consistent conceptualizations.

What: Students need ample time and practice to establish a clear and consistent description of their problem and an explanation of why it is important. Team members should be able to succinctly explain the problem and why it matters in a way that is consistent with how their teammates describe it. This becomes the value statement that your students will use to establish a consistent understanding among themselves and share with external stakeholders and potential partners.

How: There is no shortcut to writing a clear and consistent value statement. You can, however, help students recognize that writing their value statement can be broken down into steps. Use the activities at the end of this chapter (Figures 8.2 and 8.3) to walk them through the process, providing them with enough time and support to gather sufficient information and insights into the problem so that they can clearly and accurately describe why the problem matters and what might happen if nothing is done.

Students can then draft a clear and succinct value statement in the *Why does it matter?* compartment of their LCPC. You may want to let students know that developing this statement is not the end of this phase of work, but only the beginning. Students will need to practice communicating this statement to others until they are all able to represent the rationale in a consistent and coherent way.

Activities for Developing Value Statements

You can use or modify the following activities to help your students develop a strong rationale for their problem. These activities specifically aim to help students respond to the *Why does it matter?* question on their LCPC. Students should come away from these two activities able to explain why the problem matters, whom it affects, and what will happen if nothing is done about the problem.

Activity 1: Why Is This a Problem?

The purpose of this activity (see Figure 8.2) is to have students start developing their rationale for why their problem matters—specifically, clarifying why they and others think the problem they selected *is* a problem. Addressing the question *Why is this a problem?* is the first component of the more detailed value statement students will draft and record in their LCPC. Engaging in this activity will also provide legacy teams with an opportunity to test out their perspectives in relation to others'.

FIGURE 8.2
Activity: Why Is This a Problem?

Stop-Think-Do-Learn: Take your time to consider all the questions below (*stop*); generate as many possible responses as you can and select those that seem most important (*think*); share your ideas with others to get feedback (*do*); listen and learn from the feedback and make any necessary revisions to your value statement on the LCPC (*learn*).

Team Preparation

- Take 10 minutes or so to work through these questions with your legacy team:
  - What is the problem we are addressing?
  - Who is affected by this problem? Whom are we helping by solving this problem?
  - Why is this a problem? (When answering this question, focus on explaining how the problem negatively affects people.)
- As a group, take your time to develop a clear and consistent response to the above questions. Each person in your group should be able to clearly state the problem, describe who is affected by the problem, and explain why your team believes this is a problem.
- Write down your team's response in the *Why does it matter?* compartment of your team's LCPC: "This is a problem because [describe how it negatively affects people]."
- Each team member will share your team's problem and whom it affects with representatives from other teams. These representatives from other teams will have an opportunity to share why they think your team's problem matters. You will then share why your team thinks the problem matters, comparing similarities and differences between the presenting teams' and the listening teams' thoughts. This process will continue until each representative has had a chance to share his or her team's problem and received feedback on it. You will then return to your original team and revise your team's value statement as needed.

Sharing and Receiving Feedback

1. Get ready:
   - Number off in your teams.
   - Find the people from different teams who have your same number.
   - Once you have formed your new feedback team, decide the order in which you will present your legacy teams' problems. When you are not presenting, you are expected to be a member of the feedback team.
2. Presenter: Briefly explain your team's problem and whom the problem affects.
3. Feedback team: Listen carefully to the problem and whom the problem affects and think about why you think this problem matters (including the negative effect it has on people, why people should care about it, and how it affects daily life). Take 15–30 seconds to share with the presenter why you think this is a problem.
4. Presenter: As you are listening to the feedback, be sure to take notes that you can bring back to your team.
5. Presenter: Once you have heard from everyone on the feedback team, briefly share why your team thinks the problem is a problem.
6. Presenter and feedback team: Briefly note similarities or differences between the presenter's explanation of the problem, whom it affects, and why the problem is a problem and the feedback team's responses to these same questions.

Revising Your Team's Value Statement

- **Share.** In turn, team members share with their original legacy team the different perspectives they heard. As a team, be sure to note how frequently common perspectives were shared (these reinforce your team's rationale) and any interesting or important differences (i.e., things that you didn't think about but that your feedback team views as important reasons for why the problem matters).
- **Revise.** Make appropriate revisions to your team's value statement in the *Why does it matter?* compartment of the LCPC. Keep track of your revisions.

Activity 2: What Will Happen If Nothing Changes?

The purpose of this activity is to help students develop the second component of their value statement. Because this component requires forecasting, it requires teams not only to solicit their peers' perspectives but also to conduct research on perspectives beyond the classroom.

This activity, which has two parts, typically takes at least 20 to 30 minutes to complete. The first part is an in-class activity to help students develop a statement explaining what their team thinks will happen if nothing is done to address the problem and why. Here's a stem of that statement:

> If we do nothing about this problem, then we believe that it will [explain what you think will happen]. We think this will happen because [explain why you think this].

In part 1, students will work within their legacy teams to clarify their own thinking on what will happen if the problem is not addressed. They will need to consider not only the different possibilities (it will get worse, stay the same, or get better), but also the reasons behind these possibilities. Then each team member will identify at least two sources outside the classroom—family members, family friends, professionals in the community, former teachers, peers—who might know something about this problem and can share their perspective on the team member's forecast and offer their own prediction.

After discussing the various possibilities and reasons, the team will reach an agreement on a possibility and the reasons behind that possibility. Next, each team will nominate a spokesperson who will be asked to briefly share the problem with the class and what the team thinks will happen if nothing is done to address the problem and why.

In part 2 of the activity, the students from other teams will carefully consider the problem and prediction being presented, ask for clarification on anything unclear, and provide alternative possibilities and suggestions for other sources the team might consult for additional perspectives and predictions. The team members will then decide whom they might contact outside class to obtain additional perspectives and feedback.

As the teacher, you will play a key role in facilitating this process for the presenting team and the feedback teams, including establishing and reminding students of any ground rules (see, for example, Figure 6.1). It will also be important for you to share your own thoughts and perspectives to ensure that both the presenting and feedback teams benefit from the activity.

Figure 8.3 depicts one way to organize this activity. You will likely need to make adjustments to fit your students' age group and your own teaching style. The key is to have students think through what will happen if nothing is done, get feedback both in and out of class, and add a strong what-will-happen statement to the *Why does it matter?* compartment of the LCPC.

FIGURE 8.3
Activity: What Will Happen If Nothing Is Done?

Stop-Think-Do-Learn: Take your time to consider this question (*stop*); generate as many possible outcomes as you can and select those that seem most feasible (*think*); share your ideas with others to get feedback (*do*); listen and learn from the feedback and make any necessary revisions to your value statement on the LCPC (*learn*).

PART 1

Individual Preparation

- Think about the following questions: What do you think will happen if this problem is not addressed? Will it get worse, stay the same, or get better? What reasons do you have to support your answer?

- Identify at least two people outside the classroom who might know something about this problem and ask them to share their perspective on the problem and what they think will happen if nothing is done about it. Jot down some notes so you can remember what was said.

Team Preparation

- Revisit the questions as a team: What do you think will happen if this problem is not addressed? Will it get worse, stay the same, or get better? What reasons do you have to support your answer?

- Each team member shares the different perspectives he or she gathered. As a team, be sure to note how frequently common perspectives were shared (these reinforce your team's rationale) and any interesting or important differences (i.e., things that you hadn't considered when making your own predictions).

- As a team, draft your what-will-happen statement using this format:
    If we do nothing about this problem, then we believe that it will [explain what you think will happen]. We think this will happen because [explain why you think this].

- Nominate someone from your team to be a spokesperson for your group and share your what-will-happen statement with the class.

PART 2

Whole-Class Share-Out

- Presenter: Share your team's what-will-happen statement.

- Feedback teams and teacher: Let the team know if there is something that isn't clear or doesn't make sense. Provide alternative possibilities and predictions to consider. Provide suggestions for additional sources that the team might use to refine its prediction.

Revising Your Team's What-Will-Happen Statement

- As a team, discuss feedback from the whole-class share-out, consider the different perspectives surrounding your prediction, contact additional sources as needed, and make revisions to your what-will-happen statement.

- Make appropriate revisions to your team's what-will-happen statement. Keep track of your revisions.

Summing Up

Providing students with ample time to develop a rationale for why their problem matters will help solidify in students' minds that the problem they want to solve is indeed important and meaningful. As discussed in this chapter, the sessions for developing this rationale involve addressing several interrelated sub-questions. Working through these questions, students will not only clarify why the problem matters but also consider what will happen if the problem is not addressed and why addressing the problem is worth the time and effort it will take. The final value statement is a distillation of the answers to all these questions.

Arriving at this value statement requires students to collaborate and reach a shared understanding. It also requires that students refine their understanding by seeking out different perspectives and incorporating those perspectives into their arguments. You play an essential role in facilitating this work and helping students establish a clear and well-reasoned rationale.

In addition to helping students develop a clear, shared understanding of the problem, this process also helps others recognize the value of the work. This is important not only to justify the time and effort put into the legacy challenges but also to recruit support and potential partners.

Developing a rationale for their work will also prepare students for the next major milestone of the legacy challenge: developing a plan for how they intend to address the problem. This is one of the most exciting and challenging features of a legacy project and the focus of the next chapter.

9

What Are We Going to Do About the Problem?

What if your students had the opportunity not only to identify a problem but also to address it in a way that makes a positive and lasting contribution?

By now, students have had the opportunity to identify a problem, refine it, and clarify why it matters. The next step is to generate and select potential solutions to the problem—in other words, to address the question *What are we going to do about it?* on the LCPC.

The good news is that your students' previous efforts to identify, clarify, refine, and establish a rationale for their problem have likely already generated some initial ideas for how they might go about addressing the problem. The first step in addressing the problem is to pinpoint possibilities.

Pinpointing Possibilities in Legacy Challenges

Pinpointing possible ways to approach a legacy challenge requires students to address the following questions:

1. What resources do we have around us?
2. What creative combinations can we generate?
3. What solution(s) do we want to pursue?

What Resources Do We Have Around Us?

Students' first task is to step back from their problem and start identifying the various resources around them that can help them address that problem. These resources might be found in their classroom, their school, the surrounding community, and the world beyond. A resource can be a skill (e.g., the ability to sew), materials (e.g., gardening tools), a physical location (e.g., a community meeting room at the local recreation center), or any other asset that can be drawn on to benefit the work of the legacy challenge. There are likely several key resources and potential partners close at hand that students could easily overlook unless they take the time to identify and reach out to them.

There are several simple yet effective ways you can help students identify available resources (Beghetto & Breslow, 2017; Breslow, 2015). One way is to have students list all their individual strengths and assets (e.g., their own knowledge and skills, skills of people they know) and any resources they know of in their community (e.g., local businesses and organizations, public spaces).

You can also have students use Internet-based mapping tools such as Google Maps to search the surrounding area. Google Maps can provide a quick and powerful way to identify businesses and organizations (including home businesses) in the immediate vicinity of the school (Breslow, 2015) that students and teachers may not otherwise know are available.

Another way to identify resources is to use videoconferencing to connect students with experts farther afield (Townes-Young & Ewing, 2005). With the proliferation of free videoconferencing tools such as Skype, Google Hangouts, and FaceTime, experts are only an e-mail away. Students can identify and contact experts who may weigh in on their legacy projects via live video chat, recorded video messages, or even old-fashioned e-mail correspondence.

Students can also post descriptions of their projects on a website, provide access to the broader community, and request assistance in the form of both expertise and funding. Iowa BIG, the initiative-based program described in Chapter 6, uses its website to showcase project ideas and request assistance. More specifically, its "Project BBQ" website (https://projectbbq.com/BBQ/public.php) provides for each project a brief title, a thumbnail image, its topic (e.g., Education, Healthcare, Manufacturing, Human Services), and its status (either "Needs resources" or "In progress!"). Visitors to the site can click on a thumbnail image to get more information.

This type of project clearinghouse has several promising features. For one, it demonstrates at a glance the kinds of projects students are working on. It also serves as an invitation for potential partners to get involved. You can design something similar to this website to showcase the legacy projects your students are developing and identify partners who may support the project with additional resources and expertise.

To illustrate a slightly different approach, a group of students from High Tech High in San Diego, California, developed a project that involved applying their knowledge learned in health sciences class by opening and operating a food truck (Sharrock, Perry, Jacobs, & Jacobs, 2014). Even a relatively inexpensive food truck costs well over $30,000 (an insurmountable expense for most schools and traditional fund-raising efforts). Undeterred, the students shifted their focus to *external* funding and launched a Kickstarter campaign to generate the funds necessary to purchase the truck. In the end, this group of students and teachers were able to raise over $35,000 in less than six weeks to purchase the food truck.

Whichever approach students take, once they have identified available resources both in and out of the classroom, they can start generating initial ideas for how they might address their problem.

What Creative Combinations Can We Generate?

Students' next step is to generate possibilities by combining the resources they have identified with the problem they want to address. Although this may seem a bit nonsensical, combining seemingly remote or even opposite things can lead to breakthroughs. Numerous innovative solutions and scientific breakthroughs have come from what researchers call *Janusian thinking* (Rothenberg, 1996), a process named after the Roman god Janus, who can simultaneously look in two directions. Combining opposite or separate concepts can generate concepts and solutions that have *emergent properties*, or new features that aren't present in the individual concepts but only result from their combination (Sawyer, 2012). Your students can use this approach to combine apparently opposing or unrelated ideas to generate new possibilities. One way you can try this is to have students combine their problem with a seemingly unrelated interest and a community resource to create an *interest-problem-resource mash-up* (Beghetto, 2013; Beghetto & Breslow, 2017; Breslow, 2015) (see Figure 9.1).

How might this look? Let's say students have decided to tackle the growing issue of cyberbullying (problem). The students all like ice cream (unrelated interest), and there is an ice cream parlor close to their school (community resource). They try mashing up their problem, their unrelated interest, and the community resource. Although this is a seemingly random combination, the students come up with an idea for an effective solution: a restorative justice program called Ice Cream for Justice. The goal of the program is to bring together students who have been engaging in cyberbullying, their targets, and a team of student and faculty mediators in a social setting where they can eat ice cream and work through the issue.

Although some possibilities resulting from the mash-up process may turn out to be unworkable, others will point to new and powerful solutions that can be developed, implemented, and sustained. The mash-up need not always

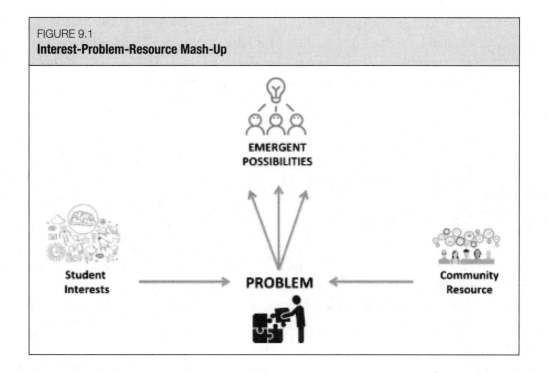

FIGURE 9.1
Interest-Problem-Resource Mash-Up

incorporate both an interest and a community resource. In some cases, just combining the problem with a community resource is sufficient. In other cases, linking a problem (e.g., providing warm clothing to families in need) with an interest (e.g., playing video games) can generate viable ideas for solutions (e.g., a video game tournament to raise money to purchase clothing for families in need). The key is to provide opportunities for students to try combining the problem they select with resources and interests to generate innovative ways of thinking about how they might address the issue.

What Solution(s) Do We Want to Pursue?

Once students have generated several possibilities for addressing the problem, they can select the most promising and viable solutions. This convergent thinking process starts with students clarifying, sharing, and receiving feedback on their potential solutions.

This step is an evaluative process that requires students to give and receive honest critiques. It is important to encourage students to freely share their ideas, no matter how unusual or seemingly silly. Sometimes the most unexpected ideas result in the most creative and effective solutions. Using group sharing ground rules, like those introduced in Chapter 6 (p. 72), can help set the expectation that students take the risk of sharing ideas while simultaneously supporting and being open to others' ideas.

This stage also benefits from seeking the perspectives of people outside the classroom to further ensure that students deeply evaluate each potential solution and converge on those that can be most feasibly and effectively implemented. Although seeking outside perspectives is not always necessary, doing so is particularly helpful when evaluating complex or technical solutions that would be enhanced by expert feedback.

During this phase, having a loopback mindset is crucial: students need to be willing to discard ideas that may not be feasible and return to generating possibilities or even rethinking the problem if necessary.

The Stop-Think-Do-Learn Connection

As with all phases of a legacy challenge, the *stop-think-do-learn* action principles play an important role in pinpointing possible solutions to the problem students have identified. Have students practice identifying when they are using these principles during the process. Figure 9.2 highlights how the action principles connect with this stage.

	FIGURE 9.2 **The Stop-Think-Do-Learn Connection: Pinpointing Possible Solutions**	
	Stop	Students stop and prepare themselves to confront the uncertainty involved in generating and selecting possibilities for addressing their problem.
	Think	Students generate multiple ideas for solving their problem, consider and evaluate these possibilities, and narrow their focus to workable solutions.
	Do	Students share and test out their ideas both inside and outside the classroom. They also give and receive feedback on possible solutions to further strengthen them.
	Learn	Students reflect on this process and make any necessary revisions to the ideas they have for addressing the problem.

 **Getting Started**

The following steps will enable you to help students generate and pinpoint possible solutions to their legacy problems.

Provide opportunities to diverge and converge.

What: Helping your students find ways to address their legacy problem boils down to providing them with time and support to cycle through various phases of divergent and convergent thinking (Guilford, 1967).

How: When engaging in divergent thinking, students should be encouraged to push themselves to generate as many ideas as possible, seek out diverse perspectives, be open to sharing and listening to unusual ideas, and keep asking the question "What if?" (Beghetto, 2016a). The goal is to generate multiple, new, and different ways of thinking about how to address the problem. As students engage in convergent thinking, they should be encouraged to seek out critiques of their ideas that are *helpful* and *actionable*. Students can shape high-quality solutions from their initial ideas if the feedback they receive is focused and strong. Rather than providing shallow or general feedback, students need to practice providing deep, specific critiques (Gibson & Mumford, 2013).

Imagine a group of students whose potential solution to their problem involves opening a student-run pop-up restaurant. A shallow, general, and unhelpful critique might be something like "Your idea will never work! A restaurant isn't like a lemonade stand. You can't just open a restaurant and serve food to people!" A more helpful and actionable critique might be something like the following:

> What kinds of things do you need to do to get the city's permission to open a pop-up restaurant? I think you probably need to get a food-handling license. Have you looked into what this requires? If not, what if you called City Hall to get some more information on it? Do you know anyone who has done this before? What if you contacted that person to ask him or her for help, too?

As students engage in convergent thinking, encourage them to retain an open and exploratory mindset (Beghetto, 2016a). The process of diverging and converging is a cycle: when evaluating ideas, students may generate new ideas, which can lead to reevaluating old ones. Moving thoughtfully between diverging and converging can help students generate viable solutions that can be refined and selected for implementation.

Hold solutions lightly.

What: Given that students will be generating and then sifting through multiple ideas to find the best solution to their problem, it is important to encourage them to discard some of their good ideas in favor of even better ones (Bilalić et al., 2008). This can be difficult when students have become attached to certain ideas. Let them know that it is OK to hold on to a possible solution—but to hold it lightly, so they can set it down if they find a better one.

How: One way to encourage this is to ask your students to come up with *too many* solutions to the problem they are trying to address. This can put your students in the proper mindset for realizing that not all the possibilities they generate will be used. This process can also help them think more flexibly when generating ideas and later be more willing to let go of good possibilities to pursue even better ones.

Don't look for perfection.

What: A good idea at hand is better than no idea at all. It is better for students to move forward with something that needs work than to spin their wheels in pursuit of a mythical "perfect" idea. A legacy challenge wouldn't be a complex challenge if it were easy to identify a solution. Encourage students to build on partial ideas rather than fixate on fully formed ones.

How: You can help students balance their pursuit of great ideas with the recognition that some potential, partially formed solutions may still be worth pursuing. This is where the notion of a "minimum viable product" (see Chapter 3)—or, in this case, minimum viable solution—can be helpful (Ries, 2011).

The key to a minimum viable solution is that students can move forward with a partial yet potentially workable solution. Once students have a chance to refine it, receive feedback, and make further revisions, they may be able to transform a tentative or incomplete idea into a strong solution (Ries, 2011).

Practice pitching to potential partners.

What: Up to this point, the legacy challenge work has primarily taken place within the classroom. Now students will begin pushing their thinking and interactions beyond the classroom walls, seeking out external feedback and partnerships. The goal of the "possibility pitch" is to provide those who are not familiar with the challenge with a concise, consistent description of the problem and an explanation of why it matters and what students intend to do about it. This way, students obtain fresh perspectives and establish potential partnerships with people and organizations that may be able to help them implement and sustain the solution.

How: When it comes to obtaining external feedback, encourage students to share their ideas with anyone who is willing to listen. Sometimes valuable input and critiques come from unexpected sources. Students should be able to clearly and coherently pitch their ideas to family members, friends, and members of the community.

The audience for the pitch is anyone who may serve as a partner because of his or her expertise or experience with the problem or potential solution. If, for instance, students are developing a program to address the social isolation of elderly community members, it would make sense for them to pitch their ideas to senior care centers and related medical and social service affiliates. You can use Activity 3 (see Figure 9.5) to give students practice developing, delivering, and refining their pitch.

. . . .

Activities for Generating and Selecting Possibilities

You can use or modify the following activities to help your students develop and refine their approach to their problem. Specifically, these activities will help students respond to the *What are we going to do about it?* question on their LCPC.

Activity 1: Generating Possibilities

The purpose of this activity (see Figure 9.3) is to have students generate possible solutions to their problem by combining ideas, seemingly unrelated interests, and resources (Beghetto, 2013, 2016d; Beghetto & Breslow, 2017; Breslow, 2015; Rothenberg, 1996). Students will also have an opportunity to share, develop, and refine any initial ideas they have for addressing their problem. Engaging in this activity prepares students for the next step, which involves evaluating their ideas and selecting the most viable solutions.

Students start out by independently listing potential resources, including skills, materials, locations, and any other assets they can draw on to solve the problem. They then share those resources with their legacy team members and broaden their search to the local community and beyond. This portion of the activity is based on related asset mapping strategies (Beaulieu, 2002; Breslow, 2015; Dorfman, 1998) and helps young people recognize that all communities and personal networks have ample assets and resources (Breslow, 2015; Kerka, 2003).

After they have identified resources, students can start generating initial solutions. Again, they will do this individually at first and then gather their ideas as a team and use the interest-problem-resource mash-up process to generate potential solutions (Beghetto & Breslow, 2017; Breslow, 2015; Rothenberg, 1996). When engaging in this activity for the first time, be sure to demonstrate the team mash-up process to the entire class so that students know what it looks like and how to proceed when working in their teams.

FIGURE 9.3
Activity: Identifying Resources

Stop-Think-Do-Learn: Take your time to consider all the resources you have or know about (*stop*); generate as many possible resources as you can (*think*); work together to create new combinations (*do*); reflect on the process and list all the new ideas you and your team have come up with (*learn*).

Individual Preparation: Identifying Individual Resources

- What are some things you know and can do well? These individual resources may encompass academics (e.g., "I'm good at math"), skills (e.g., "I'm a great cook"), and interests (e.g., "I'm an American Girl doll expert"). List these assets on a sheet of paper with your name on it or, if possible, in a shared online document that your teammates are also using.

- Think of at least three people outside this class whom you know. What can *they* do well? Again, their knowledge and skills can include anything (e.g., "My aunt is a plumber," "My neighbor owns a cupcake shop"). Add these resources to your list.

Team Preparation: Identifying Community Resources

- *Team resource identification.* Working together, use online mapping software (e.g., Google Maps) to identify a few businesses, organizations, and public locations (e.g., parks, community centers) within a 5- to 10-mile radius of your school.
  - Have one team member record the list of community resources, including a brief description of each.
  - Add this list of community resources to the list of individual resources you generated (either as a shared online document or as a written list).

- *Team resource list.* Compile a list of all the individual and community resources your team identified. Have one person on your team create a team resource list by numbering each resource that each member of your team came up with. Keeping track of the person's name will be helpful if there are any questions about the resource. For example:
  1. Cooking (De'Andre)
  2. Ice cream parlor (Rolli)
  3. Hardware store (Roxanne)

Team Problem-Resource Mash-Up

For this portion of the activity, your team will need to consult your numbered list of individual and community resources as well as your potential solutions.

- Looking at your team resource list, take turns randomly selecting one resource from the list—for example, by drawing numbers out of a hat or rolling dice.

- Working as a group, "mash up" the problem (e.g., littering) with each resource (e.g., cooking, playing video games) and come up with a solution based on that combination. See the following examples:
  - Littering in the city (problem) × cooking (resource) = "Cookout 4 Clean-Up": hosting community cookouts to raise awareness of the littering problem and establish community-based clean-up crews
  - Littering (problem) × playing video games (resource) = "Litter-Smash Go": designing a video-game app that uses location-based augmented reality to identify and remove litter throughout the town

- Make sure each person on the team has an opportunity to participate in the process.

- Continue cycling through this process until your team has generated several ideas or run out of time.

Activity 2: Selecting Possibilities

The purpose of this activity (see Figure 9.4) is to select the most feasible ideas that have been generated and start pinpointing the resources needed to implement those ideas (*What materials do we need?*). This activity is primarily a convergent thinking activity, but students should still be reminded that they are cycling through the *stop-think-do-learn* principles when engaging in it.

FIGURE 9.4
Activity: Selecting Possibilities

Stop-Think-Do-Learn: Take your time to consider all the ideas your team has generated (*stop*); consider all possibilities and select the ones you think are best (*think*); share your choices with one another (*do*); reflect on your options and decide as a team what your top solutions are and what resources you need to implement them (*learn*).

Team Idea Selection

- As a group, carefully discuss each idea—no matter how silly, wild, or impossible it seems.
  - *Find hidden strengths in seemingly weak ideas.* Discuss any strong points of seemingly weak ideas and how you can strengthen those ideas.
  - *Fix hidden weaknesses in seemingly strong ideas.* Discuss potential weaknesses of your favorite ideas and how you might address them.
- Pick your top ideas as a group.
  - You can individually vote for the ideas you think are best or discuss them as a group.
  - If you can't decide between two ideas, keep both for now and see if getting feedback on these ideas will help you decide.
- Write down your top idea(s) on your LCPC under *What are we going to do about it?*
- What kinds of resources might your team need to implement this solution? Whom can you ask to help you decide?
  - List possible contacts and needed resources on your LCPC under *What materials do we need?*

Activity 3: The Possibility Pitch

Once students have selected a tentative solution for addressing their problem, they can start to develop their possibility pitch: a clear, coherent description of their problem, why it matters, and what they intend to do about it. Each student on the team should be able to deliver this pitch. Doing so will help team members not only develop a clearer understanding of their legacy challenge but also solicit feedback from many different audiences and potential partners.

When initially giving their pitch, it is OK for students to refer to what they have recorded on their LCPC. Ultimately, however, their goal is to be able to describe their ideas without referring to a written prompt. Students will continually build on and refine their possibility pitch and, eventually, be able to describe their project's lasting contribution (see Chapter 11). They should also learn to deliver their pitch under different time constraints, including a quick 20- to 30-second "elevator" pitch and a full three- to five-minute pitch detailing the specifics.

The activity in Figure 9.5 will give students practice delivering their team's possibility pitch until they can quickly and consistently describe their ideas to others, request feedback, and build partnerships with external experts and organizations who can support the solution's development and implementation. Once teams have refined their pitch in the classroom, ask them to make a beyond-classroom pitch. You should require students to do as much of this work as possible while providing enough support that the task doesn't become

FIGURE 9.5
Activity: Developing an Initial Possibility Pitch

Stop-Think-Do-Learn: Take your time to consider how you might pitch your ideas (*stop*); generate different possibilities (*think*); provide your pitches to other teams (*do*); listen and make any necessary modifications to your ideas (*learn*).

Team Preparation

- Develop and practice your pitch. Have each member of your team practice delivering a clear and consistent description of your ideas in one minute or less.
- As a group, carefully listen to each team member's pitch and make sure he or she clearly and effectively describes the problem, why it matters, and what your team is going to do about it.
- Provide feedback to each team member to ensure that
  - Everyone delivers a pitch consistent with his or her team members'.
  - The pitch doesn't take more than one minute.
  - Everyone is ready to pitch the team's ideas to people who may not be familiar with the problem, why it matters, or what you plan to do about it.

Small-Group Practice

You will now deliver your pitch to a group made up of people from other teams.
1. Presenter: Give your pitch in one minute or less.
2. Listening group members:
   - Let the presenter know if there is something that isn't clear or doesn't make sense.
   - Describe what you liked best.
   - Provide suggestions or ideas for how the pitch or the ideas being pitched might be strengthened.
3. Presenter: Jot down the feedback and suggestions.
4. Presenter: Return to your team and share the feedback you received and any ideas that might help with revision.

Whole-Class Pitch

1. Presenting team: Nominate a spokesperson from your team to share your team's pitch with the entire class. The spokesperson provides a brief (one- to two-minute) description of your problem, why it matters, and how you plan to address it.
2. Listening teams:
   - Let the presenter know if there is something that isn't clear or doesn't make sense.
   - Describe what you liked best.
   - Provide suggestions or ideas for how the team might strengthen its pitch or the ideas being pitched.
3. Teacher: Listen for
   - Clear descriptions of the problem, why it matters, and what the team plans to do about it;
   - Feasible and logical potential solutions to the problem; and
   - Who might be a good community partner to help this team.
4. Teacher: Provide feedback that will benefit all teams.
5. Presenting team: Make any necessary revisions to your pitch.

overwhelming. Students may need your assistance identifying potential partners and contacting them to schedule the pitch, which can be done over the phone, in person, via e-mail, or through a videoconferencing tool.

Tell students to ask the following questions when making the pitch to potential partners:

- Does the problem seem like an important one?
- Do our team's possible solutions make sense to you? Do they seem feasible?

- What types of materials and support might be needed to address the problem?
- Would you be willing to provide ongoing support and, if appropriate, serve as a partner to our team?

Once all teams have pitched their ideas to someone outside the classroom, have them revisit and revise their problem statement, why it matters, and what they might do about it. Students may also be in a position to complete the *Who is helping us?* question on their LCPC. As always, they should keep a record of the old and updated versions by labeling each with a version number and date (v1.1_month_day_year).

Summing Up

The goal of this phase of work is to provide students with the time and support they need to generate possible solutions to their legacy problem. This process also includes identifying available resources that may help students implement the solution and pitching their ideas to outside audiences to obtain feedback and establish partnerships. You may find it helpful to establish time limits for students when pitching (e.g., three to five minutes for a full pitch) and receiving feedback on their solutions (e.g., 5 to 10 minutes of feedback). Establishing time limits is particularly helpful when students seek outside feedback (e.g., "Can we have 10 to 15 minutes of your time to share our idea and get your feedback?").

In some cases, it may be beneficial to have teams go through several rounds of feedback prior to selecting their idea. In other cases, teams may be ready after receiving one round of feedback to move on to planning the implementation of their solution. In still other cases, teams may require additional support or need to rethink their problem.

Before launching your first legacy challenge, it's important to decide whether you want or need to document your students' academic learning during the challenge. It is not always possible to anticipate all the things students will learn when working through a legacy challenge. Still, there are ways to "bake in" academic subject matter as well as systematically monitor what students are learning along the way. The following chapter provides ideas, insights, and tools to help you and your students document learning during legacy challenges.

10

Documenting Academic Learning in Legacy Challenges

What if you designed a legacy challenge that enabled you and your students to document academic learning along the way?

Although the primary goal of a legacy challenge is to teach students how to productively respond to uncertainty, you may simultaneously need or want to document their academic learning. Striking this balance can be tricky because it requires a shift in how we typically think about academic subject matter. When it comes to designing and implementing legacy challenges, academic content does not serve as an end but, rather, as a driving force throughout the entire process. In other words, students engaged in legacy projects put their academic learning to work in service of a meaningful challenge.

Putting Academic Learning to Work

Typically, instructional activities and tasks represent the *means* for arriving at a predetermined academic *end*. These activities don't necessarily all look the same. Two 6th grade science teachers may teach about the water cycle in different ways—one using a conventional worksheet and the other designing an elaborate, multiweek project—but in the end, both activities serve as the means to the academic end of reinforcing and assessing students' understanding of scientific concepts. By contrast, students working on a legacy project develop and use their understanding of academic subject matter as a *means* to address the problem they have identified.

Consider Winter Vincent, an elementary school student who launched a school fund-raiser to provide water filtration systems to people in need (Waves for Water, n.d.). The goal of his project was not just to learn about clean water and filtration systems (which he did), but also to come up with a way to address the problem of contaminated water. As a result, he has had a positive impact on more than 35,000 people, and his project has expanded to other schools.

Similarly, high school student Meghan Shea designed "an inexpensive water filter that removes up to 99 percent of E. coli bacteria and can be built by anyone" (Ward, 2013). Meghan had to develop and apply her understanding of scientific concepts to arrive at the solution. Again, her primary aim was not simply to learn about water filtration but to put her learning to use by solving the problem of providing affordable water filtration systems for people in need.

Dynamic Documentation in Legacy Challenges

Given that legacy challenges blend to-be-determined features with predetermined criteria and guidelines, documenting academic learning in these projects is a more complex process than it is in more conventional assignments. I recommend viewing the documentation of academic learning in a legacy challenge as a dynamic process with three requirements:

1. Anticipate what needs to be documented.
2. Document on the fly.
3. Align emergent learning with academic goals.

Anticipate What Needs to Be Documented

Anticipating what needs to be documented simply means identifying any academic skills or subject matter that students will likely need to use in their legacy challenge. You may already do this when planning learning experiences. What is different in the case of legacy challenges, however, is that the academic knowledge—rather than being the end in itself—is the means of addressing the problems students have identified. There is a degree of uncertainty because the academic skills or content needed may vary according to which problem students choose to address and the way they plan to address it. Still, you can add constraints to the legacy challenge by specifying a subject area (e.g., language arts, science, social studies, math) or skills that you would like to see students apply (e.g., persuasive writing, map reading, hypothesis testing). In other words, you can "bake in" predetermined academic content from the outset. Just make sure you allow students to determine the problem, process, and product of their legacy challenge to ensure that any predetermined academic content and skills *support* rather than overshadow the challenge.

One way to bake in this content is to introduce academic requirements at the same time as you introduce the legacy challenge to students. High school principal Sarah Mallory worked with teachers to transform her school's senior capstone project into a legacy challenge. Because the school is an arts-based magnet school, one academic requirement she included is integration of the arts (personal communication, 2017).

Mallory and her team developed a "Senior Capstone Legacy Project" manual that they use to support students in designing their legacy projects. The manual describes the defining features of a legacy challenge, outlines the nonnegotiable criteria and guidelines (e.g., the arts-based and academic subject-matter goals that need to be addressed), and includes other features tailored to the school's needs (e.g., a modified version of the LCPC with an additional compartment requiring students to explain how they will integrate the arts into their projects).

As this example illustrates, it's not difficult to incorporate predetermined academic goals that you want students to address. By building on the principles and tools introduced in this book, you and your students can customize projects according to your specific curricular needs while adhering to the defining features of a legacy challenge.

Document on the Fly

Photographers know the importance of "capturing the moment," a powerful idea that many photography companies draw on in their advertising campaigns. This concept can also be applied to the process of documenting the learning that occurs during a legacy project. Because you never know when your students will produce something surprising or powerful during the learning process, it is important to be ready to capture those moments when they arise.

How might you do this? Lisbeth Kurjiaka, a 4th grade elementary teacher, maintains a running Google Doc to record her students' and her own learning. Anytime her students produce work that she feels does a good job of demonstrating their learning in a unique or particularly effective way, she takes a photo of it, uploads it to her running record, and later adds annotations. She also uses this document to capture her own ideas, reflect on her instruction and learning, and work toward improvement (personal communication, 2017).

There are numerous free and low-cost applications that you can use to document learning on the fly. Elementary school principal Shawn Simpson encourages all the teachers and staff at his school to use the classroom communication app Classroom Dojo to capture images and stories of learning in real time. They then share these highlights with students and their families. As a principal, Simpson recognizes the importance of being able to document and celebrate moments of learning as they occur (personal communication, 2017).

You might be wondering how you can capture all this learning on your own. The good news is, you are *not* alone. You and your students can work together to keep a running record of this work. If your students have access to smart devices such as tablets or cellphones with cameras, they can easily capture images and samples of their own work and upload them to a shared document.

For instance, middle school academic dean Mark Richards developed with his team of 8th grade teachers a shared template that enables students to document and share learning on their projects. The teachers use Google Sheets because it allows separate tabs to be added at the bottom of a shared sheet. Students can then use these different tabs for daily reflections, note taking, and research compilation. Students use this template to document and share group and individual learning. Each legacy team appoints a daily scribe to enter its group report on what it accomplished on a given day under the *Daily Reflection* tab, and individual students use the *Notes* tab to record their own ideas, insights, and reflections under columns labeled with their names (personal communication, 2017).

You can build on this idea by establishing your own shared document allowing students to capture on-the-fly examples of learning that you and they can then organize and reflect on. In addition to the tools already mentioned, free tools such as Google Keep and Apple Notes provide a way to quickly collect, organize, annotate, and document example work in various formats (e.g., images, text, video, or some combination).

If your students do not have easy access to digital devices, you can achieve the same goal in an analog format—for example, by having students keep a hard-copy idea log or "innovation notebook" (L. Kurjiaka, personal communication, 2017) where they document in real time how they are applying specific academic concepts and skills. You can also maintain a physical drop box in your classroom where you and your students submit actual samples of their work, which can later be organized, digitized, and used to document the on-the-fly learning that occurs during a legacy challenge.

Regardless of how you collect artifacts of learning—digitally or physically— you and your students can later use this on-the-fly documentation to discuss, reflect on, and provide evidence of the kinds of academic concepts and skills learned and put to use throughout the course of a legacy challenge.

Align Emergent Learning with Academic Goals

The paths we end up taking in life are sometimes difficult to predict. Upon reflection, however, we are often able to see how the events of our lives connect in a coherent and meaningful way. This is because we tend to make sense of our experiences in retrospect (Weick, 1995). This is not to say we live our lives without goals or plans but, rather, that there are emergent features to the trajectories that our lives take.

The same can be said of the learning that occurs in legacy projects. Although it is possible (and sometimes necessary) to predetermine which academic standards you want students to address in a legacy challenge, some of what they learn will be difficult to predict and the connection to content standards made only in retrospect.

So, how might you align difficult-to-predict student learning in legacy projects with academic content, skills, and standards? A good way to start is to model the process of examining how the work connects to academic learning and making that connection explicit. Doing so will help your students connect the dots between what they are learning in their legacy challenge and various grade-level and subject-area standards.

For example, at Shawn Simpson's elementary school, teachers are invited to display students' academic and creative work in the hallways. With each piece is displayed a small framed informational card that describes the *who* (the author of the work), the *what* (the type of work), the *why* (the reason for doing the work), and the *standard* (the content standards the work addresses). The display, much like a museum exhibit, serves as a curation of student work. Because creative work inevitably has an emergent aspect to it, the specific standards being addressed may not always be easy to predict. By allowing for this type of alignment, students' work can maintain its emergent quality while highlighting the content standards it addresses.

Emergent learning characterizes the entire legacy challenge process, from planning and implementation to carrying the work forward from year to year. Some of this learning pertains to academic content, and some of it pertains to the process of addressing the problem students have identified.

One of the best ways to support and document such work is to use regularly scheduled check-ins. Depending on your specific goals, these check-in meetings can occur on a weekly basis and be brief (5–10 minutes) to ensure that you can check in with each of the project teams. You can also have your students keep a project journal during the week, where they can jot down ideas, keep track of how they have addressed specific project or academic goals, and raise questions to discuss at the check-in meetings.

Christine Bland, a high school gifted education resource teacher, used weekly check-ins to help her students stay on top of and learn from unexpected twists and turns that arose during the planning and implementation of an entirely student-run charity concert. These unforeseen tasks included figuring out how to schedule the event to avoid time conflicts with other events, determining which kinds of performances would be appropriate (e.g., would a heavy metal band be OK?), deciding the duration of the concert, setting admission prices, advertising the event, and planning how to recruit incoming students to carry on the work from year to year (personal communication, 2017). The result of the students' efforts was the House of Hope concert, which raises funds for women facing homelessness in their community and is now in its eighth year.

Using frequently scheduled (e.g., weekly) check-ins not only is an effective way to identify a project's emergent needs but also provides you and your students with an ideal means of documenting academic learning. One of the best ways to structure check-ins to document academic learning is to develop a simple checklist that you and your students can use to quickly record the concepts or learning standards that students have covered each week. Figure 10.1 shows a simple academic monitoring checklist covering two weeks of a project focused on providing fresh produce to families in need.

During these check-ins, you can briefly meet with students in their legacy groups, discuss what they have accomplished in the last week, and then draw from the content standards for your grade level to document what students learned or applied and how and when they did it. You can use the same checklist and approach to monitor and document subject-specific concepts and skills.

FIGURE 10.1
Academic Learning Checklist

Legacy Challenge Title: Fresh Start

	Activity	Academic Concept/Standard	Use	
			Learned About	Applied Learning
Week 1 (9/1–9/5)	Learn how to schedule and conduct Google chat with local horticulturist	• ISTE technology standards 1c and 1d: Demonstrate ability to use current technology to seek feedback	✓ (9/1)	✓ (9/3)
Week 2 (9/8–9/12)	Develop a flyer about the health benefits of fresh fruits and vegetables	• ISTE technology standards 3a, 3b, and 3d: Use research strategies to locate information, evaluate accuracy of information, and build knowledge by exploring real-world problems		✓ (9/10)
		• District ELA standards 3a and 3b: Write a factual and persuasive argument		✓ (9/12)
Notes:				

Regardless of your grade level or subject area, you can use this simple strategy to help students document the various academic concepts, skills, and knowledge that they learned and used when working on their legacy challenges. You can also use frequent check-ins to identify any gaps in what you need to cover and fill those gaps by incorporating that content into the project (e.g., providing mini-lectures, additional assignments, or academic enrichment activities).

Finally, maintaining simple running records of what students learn along the way (like the checklist in Figure 10.1) will put your students in a better position to be able to share the academic skills and knowledge they have learned and applied over the course of their legacy challenge—something they'll be doing toward the end of the project, during their public exhibition of learning (see Chapter 11).

The Stop-Think-Do-Learn Connection

Like the other phases of a legacy challenge, dynamic documentation provides ample opportunities to apply the *stop-think-do-learn* action principles. Figure 10.2 shows how the principles connect with documenting academic learning.

FIGURE 10.2
The Stop-Think-Do-Learn Connection: Documenting Academic Learning

	Stop	You and your students stop and identify the various kinds of learning that have occurred or likely will occur during the process of planning and implementing legacy challenges.
	Think	You and your students generate numerous ideas for how to document learning and then select those that make the most sense for your school and classroom context.
	Do	You and your students test out and receive feedback on the process you are using to document academic learning.
	Learn	You and your students reflect on this process, decide what works well and what needs modification, and make any necessary revisions to your approach to documenting academic learning.

Getting Started

The following steps will help you and your students document academic learning throughout the legacy challenge.

Let the problem define the content.

What: Because legacy projects are problem-driven, the ideal time to determine requisite academic skills and content is *after* students have identified the problem they want to address. In this way, the problem determines which academic skills and content are necessary rather than the academic content driving the problem. Once your students have identified a problem, you can help them align any required academic subject matter to their legacy challenge and plan how you and they will document academic learning throughout the process.

How: I'll illustrate this process with an example. Elementary school students Sara McKee and Elise Lutchman combined their interest in making "slime" with the goal of addressing the problem of affordable housing for people in their community. They developed a small business to sell their custom-made slime and donated the proceeds to a local chapter of Habitat for Humanity (Harris, 2017).

This type of project requires students to develop and apply academic skills and knowledge in at least three major subject areas: social studies (issues of affordable housing, basic economics and entrepreneurship, nonprofit organizations); math (calculating ratios and various arithmetic operations); and science (basic principles and applications of chemistry). If your students launched their own "slime for a cause" legacy project, you could help them anticipate the various academic skills and subject matter they could document and come up with a plan to capture emergent learning on the fly.

Everybody documents, and we document all the time.

What: "Everybody documents, and we document all the time" is a good slogan to adopt when working on legacy challenges. School leaders like superintendent of schools Kelly Lyman (personal communication, 2017) and building principal Mike Seal (personal communication, 2017) know how important it is to keep the process of designing and implementing complex projects manageable. Lyman has helped teachers avoid becoming overwhelmed with documentation of student learning by developing a system for teachers and students to look at student work together. Similarly, Seal, knowing that it is unrealistic to place on-the-fly documentation entirely on the shoulders of teachers, encourages teachers in his school to put some of this responsibility in the hands of students.

By establishing at the outset an ethos that "everybody documents," you and your students can become more comfortable and confident in your collective ability to connect what is being learned and applied in legacy challenges to relevant academic skills, concepts, and standards. Including your students in the process also teaches them the importance of providing evidence and clear examples of their learning, which has the added benefit of helping them see academic concepts come to life.

How: Students will, of course, need your assistance in learning how to select examples of work that demonstrate their learning and make the connection between those examples and academic standards. This requires you to set up clear routines and procedures that make sense for your own students, classroom, and school context. Regardless of whether you use digital or physical tools (or a combination of the two) to document learning, the key is to make sure you establish

- Easy methods for recording on-the-fly examples (e.g., taking cellphone photos, recording video segments, creating an idea log, keeping digital notes with Google Keep).
- Recurring and structured meetings to discuss and reflect on those examples (e.g., weekly or daily check-ins).
- Simple ways to document and align academic concepts and standards to the work students are doing (e.g., checklists like the one in Figure 10.1).

Summing Up

Although the primary goals of a legacy challenge are to provide students with an opportunity to respond productively to uncertainty and make a lasting contribution beyond the walls of the classroom, you may still need to document academic learning. With so many options now available to do so, it may feel overwhelming to pick one. Don't let this stop you. I suggest selecting an approach based on a few simple criteria:

- It is low in cost (in terms of both time and money).
- It is readily available when you need it.
- It presents a minimal interruption, allowing you and your students to quickly get back to what you were doing.

Depending on your situation, a pencil and small notebook may be all you and your students need. Regardless of which approach you choose, it should be used in conjunction with regularly scheduled check-ins and meetings so that you can help students connect what they are doing with any relevant academic concepts, skills, and standards.

Note, too, that you need not wait to launch a legacy challenge if you haven't yet developed a "perfect" approach for documenting learning; all you need is a minimum viable approach (Ries, 2011) to get started. It is only by trying out an approach that you can determine what is working well and what might need to be refined, removed, or added.

As this chapter discussed, legacy challenges can serve as vehicles for students to apply their academic knowledge in the service of making a lasting contribution beyond the walls of the classroom. In the next phase of the work, teams will plan the implementation of their solution in a way that makes a lasting impact. Students will work with outside partners to ensure that their work makes a positive contribution and prepare for a public learning exhibition to share what they learned from the process. These activities are the focus of the next chapter.

11

What Lasting Contribution Will We Make?

What if you could help your students launch a legacy project, monitor progress, share what they learned along the way, and make a lasting positive contribution?

By now, students have had an opportunity to refine their problems, generate and pitch possible solutions, gather feedback, and identify potential partners. You have decided whether and how you plan to document academic learning. It's time for students to take the major step of pushing their ideas out into the world by preparing a launch plan and working to ensure that their solution has a lasting impact.

Pushing the Work Out into the World

The goal of this phase of work is to provide students with the time and support they need to develop an action plan ensuring that their work can be successfully implemented and makes a lasting contribution. The driving questions for this phase include the following:

1. What is our launch plan?
2. What lasting impact will our work make?
3. How will we monitor progress?
4. How will we share what we have learned?

What Is Our Launch Plan?

Because launching a legacy challenge can feel overwhelming, it is important to start small by identifying a few initial steps that students can take toward their larger solution. I recommend holding frequent, brief check-in meetings with students to help them break down their projects' major goals into specific, easily monitored sub-goals that feel doable to students.

Say a legacy team is working to address the problem of homeless families' lack of access to fresh produce. The solution students decide to pursue involves developing a rooftop garden in their city—quite a formidable task. You can help students approach this challenge by developing manageable sub-goals, such as learning about the health benefits of fresh fruits and vegetables, meeting with a local horticulturist to determine what can be grown in the region, identifying a location for the garden, setting up a fund-raiser to enable the purchase of needed supplies, obtaining seeds from a local supplier, and so on.

A simple planning chart is useful for breaking down a large, complex problem into smaller tasks for students to tackle. These small steps, taken over time, will accrue until students find they have made significant headway toward meeting their larger goals. The chart in Figure 11.1 is especially helpful because it outlines *who* is doing *what* by *when* (W_3). When outlining the initial steps of a

FIGURE 11.1
Who, What, & When (W_3) Chart

Legacy Challenge Title: Fresh Start

Who	What	When	Status		
			Not started	In progress	Completed
Jasmine	Schedule Google chat with local horticulturist	September 3			✓ (9/3)
ALL	Google chat with local horticulturist	September 10			✓ (9/10)
Sarah and Anthony	Develop a flyer about the health benefits of fresh fruits and vegetables	September 17			✓ (9/15)
ALL	Meet with asst. superintendent to identify a garden location	September 24			✓ (9/24)
Paula and Jasmine	Design garden layout	October 1		✓	
ALL	Plan a fund-raiser	October 6	✓		
Notes:					

legacy project, it makes sense to start with the *what* column and list a few tasks and deadlines that need to be met before students can move on to the next steps. Students can then determine *who* will work on the task. Outlining a few steps at a time in this way works better than trying to anticipate all the necessary steps in advance. Aside from the fact that a gradual approach feels more manageable and less overwhelming, additional steps often become apparent only after the work is already under way. Having students determine three to five steps at a time makes implementation planning more feasible and flexible.

What Lasting Impact Will Our Work Make?

Once students have a plan for getting their work under way, the next question to address is *What lasting impact will our work make?* This question can be broken down into two sub-questions: *Who will carry on this work once it gets started?* and *How will we make sure that it is sustained?*

It is important to anticipate and address these questions early on to ensure that the work will continue after being passed on to a new group of students or external partners. As Laura McBain, K12 Lab Director of Community and Implementation for Stanford's design school, has explained (personal communication, 2017): a project can have a great launch and a great year—like the High Tech High food truck project described in Chapter 9—but if the next cohort of kids that inherits the project does not have the same passion for the work, it can fizzle out.

The question of who will take over and maintain the work will, of course, depend on the solution your students have developed. One way to get incoming students committed to the work is to involve them *before* handing off the project. If, for example, your students have developed a community garden, an ideal group to carry on the project would be members of next year's class. Rather than wait until the following year, your students can recruit interested students from the incoming class to participate in the work this year, before they inherit it.

Here's another example. If your students are developing an oral history project with the elders of their community, they will need to find a way to curate that material and make it accessible. This might involve partnering with the local library or museum to host an online archive of oral histories that students have collected and then passing it on to other students who can carry on the work.

A helpful way to determine the appropriate sustainability plan is to seek feedback on it from external partners (such as the library or museum, in the previous example). This not only ensures that the plan is feasible but also can result in establishing partnerships that will ensure that the work lives on.

Over time, some projects may eventually dissolve or be merged into other efforts as the situation, needs, and people involved change. Still, a key design principle of legacy challenges is to plan for ways that projects can live on, making a lasting contribution. In this way, these projects are not superficial "one-and-done" efforts that deplete the resources of communities but, rather, efforts that grow and build on healthy partnerships between schools and external partners.

How Will We Monitor Progress?

Letting students monitor their own progress empowers them to assess the impact of their efforts and, with your guidance and support, make needed adjustments along the way. As with developing a launch plan, it is important to ensure that progress monitoring is doable; again, simple tools can be powerful supports to this process. For example, students can use their W_3 charts to track what they have completed, what is in progress, and what they still need to do. Recording the dates when tasks are completed enables students to keep track of whether they are running ahead of schedule, are on schedule, or are running behind. The chart provides a quick and easy way to ensure that the work is moving forward and brings any bumps in the road to light so that they can be addressed in a timely manner.

Another quick and easy way for students to monitor progress is to keep a *legacy log*. A legacy log can be a digital or physical journal similar to the innovation notebook that Lisbeth Kurjiaka uses with her 4th grade students (mentioned in Chapter 10). Regardless of what form it takes or what you call it, the log should be a handy journal that students can easily access to jot down ideas and observations both in and out of the classroom. You can establish an expectation that students keep track of key ideas, emerging insights, and questions that arise as they work on their projects. Students can refer to their legacy logs during scheduled check-ins to provide updates and solicit feedback from you, and they can use the logs to prepare themselves for sharing their experiences in learning exhibitions down the line.

Figure 11.2 shows what a page out of a legacy log might look like, using two simple categories of entries: *Aha!* (describing any observations, learning, key moments, or insights that students believe are important to record) and *Hmm . . .* (describing any questions, concerns, stumbling blocks, setbacks, or other issues requiring further thought or assistance). This is just one example; you can structure a legacy log in whatever way makes sense for your students.

FIGURE 11.2
Legacy Log Excerpt

Sept. 10

| Aha! | I had no idea about all the different kinds of fruits and vegetables we could grow here! The horticulturist really helped us think about all the different things we could grow!

We also learned so much about what each plant needs to grow . . . including time. |

| Hmm . . . | Still not sure how we are going to decide on what to grow. So many options . . . and we really never thought about how different plants take different amounts of time to grow. Totally makes sense now, but we are now kinda stuck on what plants we want to try. . . .

The horticulturist said pick no more than four things, and she would help us, but we have to first decide. . . . |

Using simple tools like the W_3 form and a legacy log in conjunction with frequent check-ins with each team will enable you and your students to monitor and document the more informal learning and insights that students gain during the course of the legacy project.

An important aspect of progress monitoring is monitoring the *impact* projects are having. You can help students generate and seek out ideas for how they might quickly monitor whether their solution is having a positive influence. Recall from Chapter 8 the project addressing the problem of under-the-radar bullying. In that example, students could use the data they gathered from a simple, anonymous survey to establish a baseline rate of bullying experiences before they implement their solution. They can continue to administer the survey at intervals to monitor whether their efforts are having the desired effect.

As another example, consider a group of students who are developing a video and informational materials to increase local teens' awareness of the dangers of texting and driving. They can use simple metrics, like number of unique views and download counts of their materials, to get a sense of the number of people they are reaching. They can also partner with local law enforcement to monitor pre/post text-related driving citations and accident data.

How Will We Share What We Have Learned?

One of the goals of legacy challenges is to hone students' ability to communicate what they learned from the process and receive external feedback on that process. By having students publicly discuss and showcase their learning, you enable them to document that learning and make it visible in ways that go beyond typical assessments of learning (Krechevsky, Rivard, & Burton, 2009). The power of this type of learning demonstration is that it meets the "interocular traumatic test" (Edwards, Lindman, & Savage, 1963, p. 217): *it hits you right between the eyes*.

To properly prepare students for this exhibition, I recommend planning and scheduling it well in advance and letting students know about it from the outset. In addition, the various planning and implementation activities they engage in along the way—for example, keeping track of their progress and pitching their ideas to others—will also help prepare them for this learning exhibition.

Even with plenty of notice and ample preparation, some of your students may still worry that they are not ready for the learning exhibition because their work is "unfinished" or not as far along as other projects are. It is important to reassure students that it is OK—and even to be expected—that different teams will be at different stages. Some teams may have already implemented their solutions, while others are still planning their launches. Still others may have run into setbacks and returned to the planning stages.

Some of the most powerful learning emerges from the *process* of engaging with a legacy challenge—not from the final products that result from that process. In this way, whether or not a team has successfully implemented a solution, students will still have stories to tell of their process and what they learned from it. Activity 4 (pp. 133–135) provides an overview of how you can prepare students for this public exhibition.

The Stop-Think-Do-Learn Connection

Just like all phases of a legacy challenge, planning to make a lasting impact involves all four *stop-think-do-learn* action principles. Figure 11.3 highlights how this phase of work connects to these principles.

	FIGURE 11.3 **The Stop-Think-Do-Learn Connection: Making a Lasting Contribution**
Stop	Students stop and consider a possible plan for implementing their solutions and how they can ensure that those solutions will have a lasting impact.
Think	Students think of ways to break down their solutions into manageable sub-goals and consider which team members will take action on those goals and when.
Do	Students begin working toward their goals and establish a plan for monitoring their projects' progress and impact.
Learn	Students reflect on the implementation process, identify areas or steps that need refinement or revision, make any necessary changes to their plans, and present their learning at a scheduled learning exhibition.

● ●

Getting Started

The following steps will help you and your students ensure that their legacy projects make a lasting contribution.

Start small.

What: Although much can be learned from the planning that goes into a legacy challenge, the full potential of engaging with uncertainty is unleashed only once students begin implementing that plan. Although launching their projects can feel intimidating, the good news is that students don't need to take any giant leaps. On the contrary, big wins come from taking small steps (Beghetto, 2016a)—particularly when working on a legacy challenge.

The small-step approach enables students to flexibly respond to any unexpected twists and turns they encounter while implementing their solution. It also helps build students' confidence in the work and their ability to sustain the work. Researchers (Amabile & Kramer, 2011) have reported that small, consistent steps forward increase engagement, progress, and overall performance. Finally, taking small steps allows students to make small mistakes that they can quickly learn from. This can be viewed as a type of "rapid prototyping" (von Hippel, 1994) that has been attributed to successful start-ups and innovative companies (Ries, 2011).

How: You can help students keep their project goals modest by outlining and working on a few agenda items at a time using tools like the W_3 chart. Doing so will minimize the risk of large setbacks. Even when a setback takes more time to resolve (e.g., if a fund-raiser does not yield sufficient funds to purchase necessary materials), students can continue to work on other features of the challenge until they are able to regroup and establish an alternative plan (e.g., locating alternative funding sources or exploring whether less costly materials might work).

Anticipate setbacks.

What: Successful problem solvers anticipate and proactively address potential setbacks (Beghetto, 2016a; Robertson, 2017); this holds true for successful legacy challenges as well.

How: One way of building students' ability to anticipate setbacks is to have them participate in worst-case scenario exercises, such as the "premortem" (Klein, 2007). You can use the premortem to help students imagine worst-case scenarios and then pinpoint and proactively deal with potential pitfalls (see Activity 3, pp. 131–132). The purpose of this activity is to hone students' ability to identify and address "risks at the outset" (Klein, 2007, p. 18).

A major benefit of doing this work prior to implementing a solution is that it grants students "permission" to flag potential weaknesses that may otherwise go overlooked—and that students may feel reluctant to bring up. After all, once students have gotten this far into the process, they naturally feel excited and eager to implement their ideas. Students who are aware of possible pitfalls may not want to take away from the positive energy and excitement of the group. Having all students engage in a worst-case scenario activity ensures that students look for and address these potential issues before implementation.

As Shawn Simpson, the elementary principal introduced in Chapter 10, has explained, the premortem (or worst-case scenario) is a powerful way to spot issues before they arise and replaces a reactive approach with a proactive approach (personal communication, 2017). Using this technique makes students' implementation plans stronger and more likely to succeed.

Leave a lasting contribution.

What: Leaving a lasting contribution is a defining feature of legacy challenges. Students will need help from you and outside partners to establish a viable plan that ensures their work is sustained over time.

How: Leaving a lasting contribution requires providing an open, accessible record of the work your students have done. The legacy of some solutions is immediately evident. For example, restoring an old barn and turning it into a farmer's market or making the town square more welcoming by adding student-designed benches has a clear legacy because it results in a tangible product.

Finding ways to sustain and share the work of legacy challenges with less tangible products—such as the oral history project described on page 122—may require a bit more creative thought and effort. In this case, you would need to help students find a way to preserve and curate those oral histories and make them accessible to others, which might entail developing a page on the website of your school or the local history museum that includes images, text, and audio recordings. This solution would also require developing a plan to design, host, and maintain the website.

In still other cases, your students may not have been able to implement their solutions (e.g., the team ran out of time or their external partnership fell through). Even for these projects, you can stress the importance of keeping records of their plans and the progress of their work, which they may later revisit or pass on to incoming classes of students.

Finding ways to share information about legacy challenges from year to year also helps ensure that the work has a lasting impact. One of the easiest (and perhaps best) ways of doing so is to establish a webpage that houses key information resulting from your students' work from year to year. This way, all students' work—from finished, tangible products to works in progress—can be showcased and shared with others beyond the walls of the classroom. Here are some web-based examples of curated student work (both in progress and completed) to provide inspiration:

- **EdCorps**—Student-run business whose proceeds are used to support education and other community causes (http://www.edcorps.org/shop_categories/product)
- **High Tech High**—Showcase of completed projects (https://www.hightechhigh.org/student-work/student-projects)
- **Iowa BIG**—Listing of in-progress projects (https://projectbbq.com/BBQ/public.php)
- **One Stone**—Completed projects and reflections (https://onestone.org/project-good-1#archive)

Your curated site can include descriptions, links to materials, and student interviews or reflections from their learning exhibition. In this way, teachers and students from other schools, states, and even countries can learn from, replicate, and build on the work that you and your students have started.

- -

Activities for Ensuring a Lasting Legacy

You can use or modify the following activities to help students complete the *What lasting contribution will we make?* and *How are we monitoring progress and impact?* questions on their LCPCs. Students will also be able to further refine their ideas and other statements on their LCPCs. The first three activities will likely go together, and you can use the fourth at a later date, prior to a scheduled learning exhibition.

Activity 1: First Steps and Progress Monitoring

The purpose of the first activity (see Figure 11.4) is to have students use the W_3 planning form to break down the larger goals of their challenge into smaller tasks, a few at a time. After determining a few initial tasks, they can determine who will be working on each task, establish a target date for completing each task, and monitor progress along the way.

Teams begin by outlining some initial steps and determining how they will monitor their projects' progress—for example, using the W_3 chart or checking in periodically with outside experts or partners to discuss how their ideas are progressing and get timely feedback and support. You may also ask students to track their academic learning with weekly check-ins. They can record all these on their LCPCs under *Progress monitoring*.

Students will also determine how they plan to monitor their projects' impact on the target audience. Students working to reduce under-the-radar bullying, for example, might administer an anonymous survey at regular intervals to assess their project's impact. They can record this action on their LCPC under *Impact monitoring*.

After determining their initial steps, students will have an opportunity to share these ideas with you and their peers, receive feedback, and make any necessary revisions before putting their plan into action.

FIGURE 11.4
Activity: First Steps and Progress Monitoring

Stop-Think-Do-Learn: Take time to consider the team preparation questions below (*stop*); generate as many possibilities as you can before determining the answers (*think*); pick a few of your top ideas and discuss them (*do*); prepare to share them out to receive feedback and make any necessary revisions (*learn*).

Team Preparation

Working together, start planning the first steps of acting on your ideas using the W_3 planning and progress monitoring chart.

- **What?** What are a few (three to five) first steps we need to take to launch our solution?
  - Is there anything we need more information on or need to learn about?
  - Are there any people outside the class we should contact to help us take action?
  - What kinds of materials and resources do we need?

- **Who?** Who on our team can work on these tasks?
  - For each task, decide whether everyone on the team needs to help with it or one or two people can accomplish it.
  - Make sure everyone has a chance to help with the tasks.
  - Balance the work as best you can so no one is doing too much or too little.

- **When?** When is a realistic time to complete each of these tasks?
  - Be sure to give yourselves adequate time to complete these tasks.
  - Spread out the tasks over time and make sure you are not trying to do too much at once.
  - You can always finish a task early and then add the next tasks.

- How else might we monitor progress?
  - Working together and with input from your teacher, discuss how you might monitor progress (in addition to using the W_3 chart).
  - Examples include participating in weekly check-ins with your teacher and identifying some external partners who can provide feedback on your work.

- List these ideas and W_3 chart on your LCPC.
  - Once your team has completed the W_3 chart and listed some additional ways to monitor progress, you will be ready for the next activity.

Activity 2: Ensuring a Lasting Impact

The goal of this activity (see Figure 11.5) is to get students thinking about how their work will make a lasting contribution and what they need to do now to ensure that happens. It will be helpful for you to discuss with the entire class the idea of sustaining and curating the legacy projects. You can explain how you will help with this process (e.g., posting a brief description of each challenge along with student testimonials and project materials to your class or school website) and share a few ideas for how students can ensure their work continues (e.g., providing the option for next year's class to carry on the work or establishing partnerships with community organizations or groups that can help sustain the project). Teams may be in different places with their challenges, so in some cases, passing on the work might simply mean offering an idea that a new group of students can pick up to develop and implement. Students who do implement their solutions will need to find a way to ensure that the work continues after the allotted project period ends. In all cases, you want students to think about the importance of developing something that has a lasting impact and how that impact can be maintained.

FIGURE 11.5
Activity: Ensuring a Lasting Impact

Stop-Think-Do-Learn: Take time to sit with the lasting impact questions below (*stop*); generate as many possibilities as you can before determining the answers (*think*); pick a few of your top ideas and discuss them (*do*); prepare to share them out to receive feedback (*learn*) and make necessary revisions.

Team Preparation
Working together, discuss how your solution will have a lasting impact.

- How will your solution make a lasting contribution? *Take a few minutes to think about this question.*
  - Discuss all the ways you think your solution can make a lasting difference.
  - Share out your ideas and decide as a group the top few ways your solution will make a positive and lasting contribution.

- Who can help you make sure this work continues? *Take a few minutes to think about this question.*
  - How might you and your team ensure that your work continues?
  - Is this work something your team can continue to work on?
  - Can this work be passed on to the next class of students?
  - Is this work something people outside the school can help with?
  - Can this work be passed on using technology or the Internet?
  - Discuss all the different people who can help make sure the work continues.
  - Decide, as a group, who can best help ensure that your team's work lives on.

- What is your plan to make sure the work lives on? *Take a few minutes to think about this question.*
  - What are two or three things you need to do to make sure the work lives on?
  - Do you need to contact someone?
  - Do you need to develop a website?
  - What are the first couple of steps you need to take?

- Discuss all the different ways in which you can ensure that the work lives on.
  - Decide, as a group, what you think is the best way (or are the two best ways) to make sure the work lives on.

Activity 3: Worst-Case Scenario

The activity in Figure 11.6, based on Klein's (2007) premortem technique, strengthens students' ability to anticipate and proactively address potential setbacks by having them imagine worst-case scenarios. You can use this activity multiple times during action planning and implementation.

Here's how it works: Each legacy team in turn presents its solution, the initial steps it plans to take, and its ideas for ensuring the solution has a lasting impact. The teacher and the remaining teams ask clarifying questions, to which the presenting team responds. During the next portion of the activity, everyone imagines that the presenting team's plan failed and thinks of one reason why it didn't work, phrased as a "what if?" question. It may be helpful for you to provide a few examples of these questions. For example, say the presenting team is designing a garden for its legacy challenge and plans to request space for this garden from the school principal. Some "what if?" questions may include

- "What if the principal doesn't like the idea and won't give you space?"
- "What if there is nowhere near the school that has good soil to build the garden?"
- "What if the school already has a garden?"

Now let's say the team plans to pass this garden on to volunteers from the next incoming class. The following "what if?" questions demonstrate some possible pitfalls to this plan:

- "What if no one volunteers?"
- "What if some students volunteer but later change their minds and decide they don't want to work on the garden next year?"

Once students understand the process, have everyone write out their "what if?" questions and gather all the ideas in a pile. Students can use sticky notes, or you can use an electronic polling application or a shared document. You can then ask a spokesperson from the presenting team to draw one question at a time and read it aloud, and the whole class will offer feedback on how to address the issue. Keep strict time limits so that the class doesn't spend too much time on one team. You may want to break this up across a few class meetings. Be sure to help teams highlight common issues that come up, since those may point to items that need to be addressed first. If you are pressed for time, you can model the exercise for the whole class and then have each legacy team engage in this process as a team activity while you float between teams to check on the process and provide feedback.

Because presenting work to the whole class and inviting feedback requires a degree of vulnerability and risk taking from the presenting team, it's important for you to monitor and facilitate this phase carefully. Prepare students for this activity by setting clear ground rules (see Figure 7.1, p. 79) and letting them know that the point of the exercise is to imagine possible causes of the planned solution's failure—not to rip apart the project. Intervene as needed to make sure students are using "what if?" statements and sharing feasible and helpful ideas in support of the presenting team's action steps. As long as students are aware of the purpose and guidelines, the activity can be both productive and fun. When listening students point out potential issues with the sole intention of strengthening the solution, students on the presenting team will be more receptive to these ideas.

FIGURE 11.6
Activity: Worst-Case Scenario

Team Share

Each team nominates a spokesperson to quickly share its ideas and action plan (the problem, why it matters, what the team plans to do about it, and the team's planned first steps).

Presenting team: Provide a brief description of your ideas, the first three steps from your W_3 plan, and your ideas for making sure the solution has a lasting impact.

Listening teams and teacher:
- Listen for anything that is not clear or doesn't make sense.
- Ask for clarification on anything that is unclear (but do not provide feedback yet).

Presenting team: Answer the questions, clarifying any unclear points and providing more information as needed.

What If?

Everyone participates in this part of the activity, including the presenting team, the listening teams, and the teacher.

- Imagine that the presenting team takes the steps it described, and it is a complete disaster.
- Think about one reason why some part of the plan didn't work.
- Write out this reason in the form of a "what if" question ("What if your team . . . ?").

Worst-Case Problem Solving

A spokesperson from the presenting team draws one "what if?" question at a time, reads it aloud, and then discusses with the whole class how the issue might be solved, using the action principles:
- **Stop** and listen carefully about the issue.
- **Think** about potential ways to address the issue.
- **Do** by sharing ideas for how to address the issue.
- **Learn** by reflecting on these ideas and deciding on revisions.

Making Necessary Revisions

- Based on the feedback your team received, make any necessary revisions to your W_3 chart.
- Keep a record of changes by labeling each version with a number and date (e.g., v1.1_month_day_year).

Activity 4: Learning Exhibition Guidelines

The ultimate goal of a legacy challenge is not for students to come up with a perfect solution to a problem and achieve a successful outcome to their efforts but, rather, to give students an opportunity to publicly share what they learned from the process of engaging with uncertainty. The purpose of this public exhibition is to make "learning visible" (Krechevsky et al., 2009) to you, to students, to their peers, to their families, and to the larger community.

Although you will likely modify the guidelines for this presentation (see Figure 11.7) to suit your students' and your needs, they represent one way to prepare and carry out a successful exhibition of learning. You can, of course, remove or add items, such as specific content standards or other aspects you want students to reflect on and discuss.

The activity in Figure 11.7 is designed to allow for brief but insightful presentations that can be followed by a Q&A session or a gallery walk (e.g., people stopping by team tables to discuss the work further). The guidelines break down the presentation into two parts, for a total time of 10 minutes. Part 1 provides a brief overview of students' legacy challenge, highlighting the most recent version of the key elements outlined on their LCPC. Students can use the LCPC as a handy resource when they prepare for the presentation and practice discussing the key features of their challenge, but they should avoid reading from it during the presentation.

Part 2 focuses on what students learned from the process. It is organized using the *stop-think-do-learn* action principles and aims to provide a behind-the-scenes look at key moments when students used these principles to address their legacy challenge. Even students who haven't yet implemented their solution can present their process to that point. The goal is to have them discuss their efforts, especially the messiness of dealing with uncertainty, setbacks they encountered, whether they overcame those setbacks, and what they learned along the way.

Note that the guidelines ask students to use a "physical metaphor"—an object, an image, or a movement to help tell the story of their process. Using objects as metaphors is a powerful way to communicate key themes of your students' experience with their legacy challenges. Indeed, this use of objects can lend visual clarification to people's feelings, experiences, thoughts, and decision making across various settings (Franklin, 2015; Hoskins, 1998; Woodside, 2004). In the case of the learning exhibition, students use a physical metaphor to represent their experiences with the process, including how their conceptions of the problem and solution changed as a result of working through the process.

FIGURE 11.7
Activity: Learning Exhibition Guidelines

Stop-Think-Do-Learn: Take time to carefully review and explore how your team will meet the requirements of each part of this presentation (*stop*); generate as many ideas as possible for how to demonstrate what you learned from the process and select a few ideas that you agree on as a team (*think*); test out these ideas by practicing your presentation and getting feedback from your teacher and others (*do*); reflect on the feedback and make necessary revisions to your presentation (*learn*).

Team Planning

Working together, determine how you will demonstrate what you learned from the legacy challenge process. *Note:* Make sure everyone on your team plays some role in both parts of the presentation. Have fun and learn from one another!

Part 1: Overview of Your Challenge (2–3 minutes)

Working as a team, decide who will describe each of the following aspects of your challenge to the audience:

- *The problem and why it matters:* Briefly describe your team's problem, why it matters, and whom it impacts.

- *What you're doing about it:* Describe the solution you developed to address this challenge.

- *Steps taken:* Describe whether you have taken steps to implement this solution.

- *External partners:* Describe who is helping you in this process.

- *Progress monitoring:* Describe how your team is monitoring progress and the impact of your work.

- *Lasting impact:* Describe how you will make sure your work moves forward and makes a lasting contribution.

Part 2: A Metaphor for Learning (7–8 minutes)

You will be using a physical metaphor (object, image, or movement) to illustrate your group's experience using the action principles to address your complex challenge and what you learned from the process. *Note:* You can use one or more objects, images, or movements to serve as your physical metaphor (e.g., different stages of a block of clay being transformed into a sculpture).

- **Stop.** Use a physical metaphor (object, image, or movement) to help you describe some key moments when your team faced uncertainty (e.g., finding a problem, coming up with solutions, trying to implement your solutions). This can include fears or concerns that you addressed as part of sitting with the uncertainty of the problem.

- **Think.** Use your physical metaphor to demonstrate some key moments you and your team had with generating possibilities and selecting the best ones. This might be when something major changed (e.g., your problem or planned solution) or any other key moments coming up with and selecting ideas for your problem or solution.

- **Do.** Again, use the physical metaphor to help you highlight some key moments in your team's experience developing a plan of action and trying to implement your solution. You can highlight setbacks you experienced, times when you might have needed to change directions, or anything that has to do with planning and trying to actually solve the challenge—even it if didn't work out or you are currently stuck. It is also OK if your team hasn't gotten to this point yet; you can still use the object, image, or movement to discuss your ideas for taking first steps toward implementing your solutions.

- **Learn.** Use the physical metaphor to help you demonstrate or describe what you and your team learned from this process. Here are some questions you can address in this part of the presentation:
  - *What have you learned about this problem?*
  - *What have you learned about trying to solve a problem like this?*
  - *What kinds of academic skills did you use or have to learn?*
  - *What have you learned about your team?*
  - *What have you learned about yourself?*

- **Connect the dots.** You (and your team) will be expected to make some brief final comments about how your physical metaphor tells the story of your process.

For example, students might use a Slinky to illustrate how they had to move together when using the four action principles to address their legacy challenge. During rough spots or when they were out of sync as a team, they came to a standstill, just as a Slinky sometimes gets stuck on a step on its way down a staircase. When this happened, students sought out their teacher or an outside partner to give them a little nudge forward until they were once more able to move toward implementing their solution.

I recommend curating artifacts from students' learning exhibitions on a classroom or school website to give future students an idea of what these presentations look like and to push the learning out into the world. You can, for instance, upload pictures of the physical metaphors that teams used in their presentations and have teams provide a brief explanation of their legacy challenge and what the metaphors represent. The website serves as a curated showcase of students' hard work that anyone can visit and revisit.

Summing Up

Both you and your students play an important role in ensuring that their work makes a positive and lasting contribution. Although the specifics for each challenge may vary depending on how much work students are able to accomplish in the allotted time, you can still ensure that each solution has an impact by curating and sharing the key features of each project.

A simple but powerful way of doing so is to dedicate a web page to legacy challenges on your classroom or school website. You can upload students' LCPCs as well as any other materials, images, and student testimonials. This gallery of projects can be organized by year or even topic area. The key is to make it accessible beyond the walls of your classroom so that other teachers and students in your building, district, and beyond can learn from, replicate, and build on the work your students have done.

Ideally, your students will develop at least a few solutions that continue beyond the project's time span. In some cases, students may develop a challenge that they continue to work on even as they move from one grade to the next— for example, a T-shirt business that uses T-shirts as a medium to communicate historical facts about students' town or state.

In other cases, you and your students may need to develop a succession plan to pass the work on to the next class. For example, 6th graders who started a community lending library in partnership with a local used bookstore can involve interested 5th graders, who then continue managing the lending library once they become 6th graders and eventually pass it on to the next cohort of students.

As is the case with most complex challenges, clarifying the specifics of how to implement and sustain the work is part of the process. The plan and process will differ for each challenge and will need to be addressed by students working together and in collaboration with external partners to generate ideas, test those ideas, and make modifications along the way.

You will play a key role in helping students develop the confidence and competence necessary to work through the various mini-challenges and problems they encounter as they attempt to address the larger complex challenge of responding productively to the uncertainty they face.

Finally, students will demonstrate what they learned in a public exhibition of learning. This is an opportunity for students to share the behind-the-scenes story of their process, how they used the action principles to address the uncertainty they faced, and what they learned along the way.

Final Thought

The central argument of this book is that students need opportunities to productively respond to uncertainty. They also need structure and support to do so. The ideas and tools I have presented are intended to help you find ways to simultaneously support and challenge students, including helping them push their learning beyond the walls of the classroom with ambitious legacy challenges.

I encourage you to trust yourself and your students to take the leap and see how complex challenges can awaken productive problem solving in and beyond your classroom. I'm confident that you will be surprised at what you and your students are capable of accomplishing.

The first step is to ask, *What if?*

What if you started today by transforming a routine activity into a more complex one? What if you used complex challenges to unleash students' learning, problem solving, and creativity? What if you embarked on a legacy challenge with your students?

You'll never know the answers to these questions unless you have the courage to try.

FAQs
Complex Challenges in and Beyond the Classroom

Q. How can I use complex challenges in my teaching if there is no room in my curriculum to add something new?

A. Incorporating complex challenges in your classroom does not necessarily require more time. Rather, it is about using the time you already have differently. Chapter 3 highlights ways you and your students can restructure existing assignments and tasks into moderate and complex challenges.

Legacy challenges do take more time. They can, however, be broken down into mini-sessions that can be incorporated into your existing curriculum by using smaller blocks of time (see Chapter 5).

Q. Is it better to have an entire class or small groups work on a legacy challenge?

A. Although having an entire class work on a challenge can be easier to manage, it can undermine students' motivation because they are being required to address the same problem. That said, if students have a voice in selecting the problem and all students endorse the problem selected, then using one legacy challenge for the entire class can work (especially if it is a small class).

Q. How can I use complex challenges in my teaching when assignments are predetermined by the adopted curriculum of my school or district?

A. You can use complex challenges by changing the way you use those predetermined assignments. For example, let's say your school district adopted a math curriculum that followed the standard process of requiring teachers to introduce concepts, problems, and procedures from the text; demonstrate how to solve problems by walking students through worked examples; and then assign predetermined worksheets in class and as homework. Teachers are required to use all the practice worksheets with students to ensure fidelity to the curriculum. Doing so, however, leaves no time for "extra" or teacher-made assignments in math. How might you still use the worksheets, but in a way that opens up time in your curriculum for complex challenges?

One way is to use the worksheets during the time allotted for "worked examples." You can work through them together as a class. This frees up "practice time" for students to work on more complex challenges. It also provides the option to do the homework during class and assign moderately complex challenges for homework.

By creatively rethinking how you use time and materials, you likely will find ways to incorporate complex challenges within the curricular constraints you face.

Q. How often should I use these different types of challenges in my classroom?
A. Ideally, for every topic you teach, your students should have a chance to experience the full spectrum of challenges (from simple to complex). Although there is no magic distribution, you might start by using simple and moderate challenges most frequently and complex challenges somewhat less frequently.

As you systematically use these different types of challenges in your classroom, you will start to develop a better sense of whether the distribution makes sense for the topic you are teaching, the time you have, and your students' needs.

The key is to provide students with an opportunity to engage with moderate and complex challenges for every topic you teach, with the goal of preparing them to move into increasingly complex challenges. Chapters 2 and 3 provide insight into how you can strike that balance in your classroom, and Chapters 5 through 11 help you prepare for legacy challenges.

Q. Should I use complex challenges as homework assignments?
A. It depends. Using complex challenges as homework can be tricky. Generally speaking, starting and completing a complex classroom challenge entirely as a homework assignment should be avoided.

When students work on complex classroom challenges at home, they may get overwhelmed. If you do assign complex challenges as homework, make sure that you provide clear expectations to your students, explaining that they can work on but need not finish these challenges at home. You can then provide needed assistance and support when they return to class.

For longer complex challenges like legacy challenges, it is certainly possible and appropriate to assign portions as homework. The key is making sure that students have access to necessary supports and options to get assistance.

Various online technologies—like wikis, Google Docs, and other collaboration tools—can provide such support, allowing students to post questions, share ideas, seek input from you and peers, and collaborate with one another. For such tools to be useful, you and your students will need to actively monitor and use them.

Q. Should I use complex challenges for my strongest students and use simpler or more moderately challenging problems for everyone else?

A. The goal is to provide *all* students with opportunities to respond productively to uncertainty. Legacy challenges provide an ideal vehicle for students at all levels to participate because students will be working in teams and seeking outside assistance as needed.

Individual classroom challenges, which tend to be more academically oriented, are a bit different. Students need to have the requisite academic skills and knowledge to engage with complex classroom challenges independently, or they will likely be frustrated. It's important to provide students with challenges that allow them to productively grapple with the work without getting overwhelmed (or underwhelmed) by it.

That said, you should give all students an opportunity to strive for more complex challenges. Doing so may require you to provide additional time and instructional support, but you should be helping them move from simple to more complex classroom challenges. Moreover, all students benefit from recognizing when they need more support and when they are ready for a more challenging experience. Chapter 3 highlights ideas for adding and removing complexity as needed.

It is also worth noting that competence is domain-specific (Alexander et al., 2009). In the context of complex challenges, students' competence can also be task-specific. Consequently, it is important to avoid using general, fixed categories in our appraisals of students (e.g., "She's very creative," "He is a weak student," or "She's outstanding at math").

Even a seemingly strong student may struggle with a complex challenge if he or she does not have the requisite prior knowledge, whereas a seemingly "weak" student may shine on that same challenge. The key is recognizing that competence in the context of complex challenges is dynamic and can and *should* be adjusted to ensure that students can learn how to productively respond to the uncertainty they face (rather than get demoralized by it).

Q. Can legacy challenges be used with younger students?

A. As this book shows, legacy challenges can certainly be used with younger students. Examples of legacy projects led by young students include everything from saving endangered species of shrimp to publishing an article in a top scientific journal. The key consideration when using legacy challenges with younger students is that they will need more support. You'll need to modify the wording of the activities included in this book, make sure to break down the work into smaller chunks, and partner with outside experts who can provide additional structure and guidance.

With requisite instructional support and encouragement, even early elementary students can develop confidence and competence tackling the uncertainty of complex challenges, including legacy challenges. Just like anything, when using complex challenges with younger students, you will need to find ways to make the experience accessible and beneficial for your particular population of students. The best way to determine what your students can do is to let them try.

References

Alexander, P. A., Schallert, D. L., & Reynolds, R. E. (2009). What is learning anyway? A topographical perspective considered. *Educational Psychologist, 44,* 176–192.

Amabile, T. M. (1996). *Creativity in context: Update to* The Social Psychology of Creativity. Boulder, CO: Westview Press.

Amabile, T., & Kramer, S. J. (2011). *Using small wins to ignite joy, engagement, and creativity at work.* Cambridge, MA: Harvard Business Review Press.

Bandura A. (1997). *Self-efficacy: The exercise of control.* New York: Freeman.

Bandura, A. (2006). Guide for constructing self-efficacy scales. In F. Pajares & T. Urdan (Eds.), *Self-efficacy beliefs of adolescents* (pp. 307–337). Greenwich, CT: Information Age.

Beaulieu, L. J. (2002). *Mapping the assets of your community: A key component for building local capacity.* Mississippi State, MS: Southern Rural Development Center. Retrieved from https://files.eric.ed.gov/fulltext/ED467309.pdf

Beghetto, R. A. (2013). *Killing ideas softly? The promise and perils of creativity in the classroom.* Charlotte, NC: Information Age Press.

Beghetto, R. A. (2016a). *Big wins, small steps: Leading for and with creativity.* Thousand Oaks, CA: Corwin.

Beghetto, R. A. (2016b). Leveraging micro-opportunities to address macroproblems: Toward an unshakeable sense of possibility thinking. In D. Ambrose & R. J. Sternberg (Eds.), *Creative intelligence in the 21st century: Grappling with enormous problems and huge opportunities* (pp. 159–174). Rotterdam, the Netherlands: Sense.

Beghetto, R. A. (2016c). Creativity and conformity. In J. A. Plucker (Ed.), *Creativity and innovation: Current understandings and debates* (pp. 267–275). Waco, TX: Prufrock.

Beghetto, R. A. (2016d). Learning as a creative act. In T. Kettler (Ed.), *Modern curriculum for gifted and advanced learners* (pp. 111–127). Waco, TX: Prufrock.

Beghetto, R. A. (2017a). Legacy projects: Helping young people respond productively to the challenges of a changing world. *Roeper Review, 39,* 1–4.

Beghetto, R. A. (2017b). Inviting uncertainty into the classroom. *Educational Leadership, 75*(2), 20–25.

Beghetto, R. A. (2017c). Lesson unplanning: Toward transforming routine problems into non-routine problems. *ZDM: The International Journal on Mathematics Education, 49*(7), 987–993.

Beghetto, R. A., & Breslow, J. Z. (2017). Creativity strategies. In K. Peppler (Ed.), *The SAGE encyclopedia of out-of-school learning.* Thousand Oaks, CA: Sage.

Beghetto, R. A., & Dilley, A. E. (2016). Creative aspirations or pipe dreams? Toward understanding creative mortification in children and adolescents. In B. Barbot (Ed.), *Perspectives on creativity development. New Directions for Child and Adolescent Development, 151,* 79–89.

Beghetto, R. A., & Kaufman, J. C. (2007). Toward a broader conception of creativity: A case for "mini-c" creativity. *Psychology of Aesthetics, Creativity, and the Arts, 1,* 73–79.

Bilalić, M., McLeod, P., & Gobet, F. (2008). Why good thoughts block better ones: The mechanism of the pernicious Einstellung (set) effect. *Cognition, 108,* 652–661.

Blackawton, P. S., Airzee, S., Allen, A., Baker, S., Berrow, A., Blair, C., et al. (2011). Blackawton bees. *Biology Letters, 7,* 168–172.

Boss, S. (2015). *Real-world projects: How do I design relevant and engaging learning experiences? (ASCD Arias).* Alexandria, VA: ASCD.

Boss, S. (2017). Partnership strategies for real-world projects [Blog post]. *Edutopia.* Retrieved from https://www.edutopia.org/blog/partnership-strategies-real-world-projects-suzie-boss

Brasof, M. (2015). *Student voice and school governance: Distributing leadership to youth and adults.* New York: Routledge.

Breslow, J. Z. (2015). *The community creativity collective: Introducing and redefining a community-based model for creative curriculum development* (doctoral dissertation). Available from ProQuest Dissertation and Theses database (UMI 3700432).

Brophy, S., Klein, S., Portsmore, M., & Rogers, C. (2008). Advancing engineering education in P12 classrooms. *Journal of Engineering Education, 97,* 369–387.

Brown, T. (2009). *Change by design: How design thinking transforms organizations and inspires innovation.* New York: HarperCollins.

Chaudron, C. (2014). *Power in the process.* Retrieved from http://www.punahou.edu/news/item/index.aspx?LinkId=2759&ModuleId=161

Cheon, S. H., & Reeve, J. (2015). A classroom-based intervention to help teachers decrease students' amotivation. *Contemporary Educational Psychology, 40,* 99–111.

Chou, E. Y., Halevy, N., Galinsky, A. D., & Murnighan, J. K. (2017). The Goldilocks contract: The synergistic benefits of combining structure and autonomy for persistence, creativity, and cooperation. *Journal of Personality and Social Psychology, 113,* 393–412.

Csikszentmihalyi, M., & Sawyer, K. (1995). Creative insight: The social dimension of a solitary moment. In R. J. Sternberg & J. E. Davidson (Eds.), *The nature of insight* (pp. 329–363). Cambridge, MA: MIT Press.

Davidson, J. E. (2003). Insights and insightful problem solving. In J. E. Davidson & R. J. Sternberg (Eds.), *The psychology of problem solving* (pp. 149–175). Cambridge, UK: Cambridge University Press.

Dorfman, D. (1998). *Mapping community assets workbook. Strengthening community education: The basis for sustainable renewal.* Portland, OR: Northwest Regional Educational Laboratory. Retrieved from https://files.eric.ed.gov/fulltext/ED426499.pdf

Edwards, W., Lindman, H., & Savage, L. J. (1963). Bayesian statistical inference for psychological research. *Psychological Review, 70,* 193.

Ericsson, K. A., Krampe, R. T., & Tesch-Römer, C. (1993). The role of deliberate practice in the acquisition of expert performance. *Psychological Review, 100,* 363–406.

Flatow, I. (1992). *They all laughed . . . From light bulbs to lasers: The fascinating stories behind the great inventions that have changed our lives.* New York: HarperCollins.

Franklin, P. (2015). Tell me all about it: Using objects as metaphors. In C. F. Sori, L. Hecker, & M. E. Bachenberg (Eds.), *The therapist's notebook for children and adolescents: Homework, handouts, and activities for use in psychotherapy* (2nd ed.) (pp. 9–12). New York: Routledge.

Fulmer, S. M., & Turner, J. C. (2014). The perception and implementation of challenging instruction by middle school teachers: Overcoming pressures from students. *The Elementary School Journal, 114,* 303–326.

Gettinger, M., & Kohler, K. M. (2006). Process-outcome approaches to classroom management and effective teaching. In C. M. Evertson & C. S. Weinstein (Eds.), *Handbook of classroom management: Research, practice, and contemporary issues* (pp. 73–95). New York: Routledge.

Getzels, J. W. (1964). Creative thinking, problem solving, and instruction. In E. R. Hilgard (Ed.), *Theories of learning and instruction* (pp. 240–267). Chicago: University of Chicago Press.

Getzels, J. W., & Csikszentmihalyi, M. (1966). Portrait of the artist as an explorer. *Trans-action, 3*, 31–34.

Gibson, C., & Mumford, M. D. (2013). Evaluation, criticism, and creativity: Criticism content and effects on creative problem solving. *Psychology of Aesthetics, Creativity, and the Arts, 7*, 314–331.

Girlshealth.gov. (2016). *2016 Spotlight: Trisha Prabhu*. Retrieved from https://www.girlshealth.gov/spotlight/2016/6.html

Godin, S. (2015). *Poke the box: When was the last time you did something for the first time?* New York: Penguin.

Graham, D. A. (2010). Silly ideas that made millions. *Newsweek*. Retrieved from http://www.newsweek.com/silly-ideas-made-millions-69107.

Guilford, J. P. (1967). *The nature of human intelligence*. New York: McGraw-Hill.

Harris, S. (2017). *Getting slime-y for a good cause*. Retrieved from https://www.habitathm.ca/single-post/2017/07/10/Getting-Slime-y-For-a-Good-Cause

Harvard-Smithsonian Center for Astrophysics (Producer). (2000). *Private universe project in mathematics* [DVD]. Retrieved from http://www.learner.org/resources/series120.html?

Hoskins, J. (1998). *Biographical objects: How things tell the stories of people's lives*. New York: Routledge.

Iowa BIG. (n.d.). *Iowa BIG outcomes*. Retrieved from http://www.iowabig.org/wp-content/uploads/2014/11/Iowa-BIG-Outcomes.pdf

Jang, H., Reeve, J., & Deci, E. L. (2010). Engaging students in learning activities: It is not autonomy support or structure, but autonomy support and structure. *Journal of Educational Psychology, 102*, 588–600.

Juliani, A. J. (2014). *Inquiry and innovation in the classroom: Using 20% time, genius hour, and PBL to drive student success*. New York: Routledge.

Kamii, C. (2000). *Double-column addition: A teacher uses Piaget's theory* [Video]. New York: Teachers College Press.

Kaufman, J. C. (2016). *Creativity 101* (2nd ed.). New York: Springer.

Kaufman, J. C., & Beghetto, R. A. (2013). In praise of Clark Kent: Creative metacognition and the importance of teaching kids when (not) to be creative. *Roeper Review, 35*, 155–165.

Kerka, S. (2003). Community asset mapping. *Clearinghouse on Adult, Career, and Vocational Education: Trends and Issues, 47*, 1–2.

Klein, G. (2007). Performing a project premortem. *Harvard Business Review, 85*, 18–19.

Kozbelt, A., Beghetto, R. A., & Runco, M. A. (2010). Theories of creativity. In J. C. Kaufman & R. J. Sternberg (Eds.), *Cambridge handbook of creativity*. New York: Cambridge University Press.

Krechevsky, M., Rivard, M., & Burton, F. R. (2009). Accountability in three realms: Making learning visible inside and outside the classroom. *Theory Into Practice, 49*, 64–71.

Kuhn, D. (2000). Metacognitive development. *Current Directions in Psychological Science, 9*, 178–181.

Lee, H. S., & Anderson, J. R. (2013). Student learning: What has instruction got to do with it? *Annual Review of Psychology, 64*, 445–469.

Lesgold, A. M. (1988). Problem solving. In R. J. Sternberg & E. E. Smith (Eds.), *The psychology of human thought* (pp. 188–213). New York: Cambridge University Press.

Levenson, E. (2011). Exploring collective mathematical creativity in elementary school. *Journal of Creative Behavior, 45*, 215–234.

Littleton, K., & Mercer, N. (2013). *Interthinking: Putting talk to work*. London: Routledge.

Lubart, T. I. (2001). Models of the creative process: Past, present and future. *Creativity Research Journal, 13*, 295–308.

Mackworth, N. H. (1965). Originality. *American Psychologist, 20*, 51–66.

Maurya, A. (2012). *Running lean* (2nd ed.). Sebastopol, CA: O'Reilly Media.

Mumford, M., & McIntosh, T. (2017). Creative thinking processes: The past and the future. *Journal of Creative Behavior, 51*, 317–322.

National Public Radio. (2016, September 9). Teen creates "sit with us" app for bullied kids [Transcript]. *All Things Considered.* Retrieved from http://www.npr.org/2016/09/09/493319114/teen-creates-sit-with-us-app-for-bullied-kids

Nelson, N., Malkoc, S. A., & Shiv, B. (2018). Emotions know best: The advantage of emotional versus cognitive responses to failure. *Journal of Behavioral Decision Making, 31*(1), 40–51.

Newell, A., & Simon, H. A. (1972). *Human problem solving.* Upper Saddle River, NJ: Prentice Hall.

Niu, W., & Zhou, Z. (2017). Creativity in mathematics teaching: A Chinese perspective (an update). In R. A. Beghetto & J. C. Kaufman (Eds.), *Nurturing creativity in the classroom* (2nd ed.) (pp. 86–107). New York: Cambridge University Press.

One Stone. (2016, May 14). *Lean on me.* Boise, ID: Author. Retrieved from http://onestone.org/portfolio_page/lean-on-me2016/

Plucker, J., Beghetto, R. A., & Dow, G. (2004). Why isn't creativity more important to educational psychologists? Potential, pitfalls, and future directions in creativity research. *Educational Psychologist, 39*, 83–96.

Pólya, G. (1966). On teaching problem solving. *Conference Board of the Mathematical Sciences, The role of axiomatics and problem solving in mathematics* (pp. 123–129). Boston: Ginn.

Pretz, J. E., Naples, A. J., & Sternberg, R. J. (2003). Recognizing, defining, and representing problems. In J. E. Davidson & R. J. Sternberg (Eds.), *The psychology of problem solving* (pp. 3–30). New York: Cambridge University Press.

Reeve, J. (2009). Why teachers adopt a controlling motivating style toward students and how they can become more autonomy supportive. *Educational Psychologist, 44*, 159–175.

Reeve, J., & Tseng, C. M. (2011). Agency as a fourth aspect of students' engagement during learning activities. *Contemporary Educational Psychology, 36*, 257–267.

Renzulli, J. S., Gentry, M., & Reis, S. M. (2004). A time and a place for authentic learning. *Educational Leadership, 62*, 73–77.

Ries, E. (2011). *The lean startup: How today's entrepreneurs use continuous innovation to create radically successful businesses.* New York: Crown Business.

Robertson, S. I. (2017). *Problem solving* (2nd ed.). New York: Routledge.

Rogers, L. (1996). *The California shrimp project: An example of environmental project-based learning.* Berkeley, CA: Heyday Books.

Root-Bernstein, R., & Root-Bernstein, M. (2017). People, passions, problems: The role of creative exemplars in teaching for creativity. In R. A. Beghetto & B. Sriraman (Eds.), *Creative contradictions in education* (pp. 143–180). Switzerland: Springer.

Rosiek, J., & Beghetto, R. A. (2009). Emotional scaffolding: The emotional and imaginative dimensions of teaching and learning. In M. Zembylas & P. A. Shutz (Eds.), *Advances in teacher emotion research* (pp. 175–194). New York: Springer.

Rothenberg, A. (1996). The Janusian process in scientific creativity. *Creativity Research Journal, 9*, 207–231.

Rothenberg, A. (2014). *Flight from wonder: An investigation of scientific creativity.* New York: Oxford University Press.

Ryan, R. M., & Deci, E. L. (2006). Self-regulation and the problem of human autonomy: Does psychology need choice, self-determination, and will? *Journal of Personality, 74*, 1557–1586.

Sabatier, J. (2016). Beaverton 8th grader's project wows at Google Science Fair [Blog post]. *Oregon Public Broadcasting.* Retrieved from http://www.opb.org/radio/article/bandage-oregon-student-google-science-fair/

Sawyer, R. K. (2012). *Explaining creativity: The science of human innovation* (2nd ed.). New York: Oxford University Press.

Schoenfeld, A. H. (1983). The wild, wild, wild, wild, wild world of problem solving (A review of sorts). *For the Learning of Mathematics, 3*, 40–47.

Schoenfeld, A. H. (2015). Thoughts on scale. *ZDM: The International Journal on Mathematics Education, 47*, 161–169.

Schraw, G. (1998). Promoting general metacognitive awareness. *Instructional Science, 26*, 113–125.

Sharrock, D., Perry, L., Jacobs, G., & Jacobs, J. A. (2014, Spring). A reel-y authentic project. *UnBoxed: A Journal of Adult Learning in Schools, 11*. Retrieved from http://gse.hightechhigh. org/unboxed/issue11/a_reel-y_authentic_project/

Stanton, T. K., Giles, D. E., & Cruz, N. I. (1999). *Service-learning: A movement's pioneers reflect on its origins, practice, and future.* San Francisco: Jossey-Bass.

Stein, M. I. (1953). Creativity and culture. *Journal of Psychology, 36*, 311–322.

Sternberg, R. J., & Lubart, T. I. (1995). *Defying the crowd: Cultivating creativity in a culture of conformity.* New York: Free Press.

Stone, M. K., & Barlow, Z. (2010). Social learning in the STRAW project. In A. E. J. Wals (Ed.), *Social learning towards a sustainable world* (pp. 405–418). The Netherlands: Wageningen Academic.

Townes-Young, K. L., & Ewing, V. R. (2005). NASA Live creating a global classroom: A NASA videoconferencing program knocks down traditional educational boundaries, drawing together teachers, students, and field experts in a single virtual setting for the benefit of all. *THE Journal, 33*, 43.

Von Hippel, E. (1994). "Sticky information" and the locus of problem solving: Implications for innovation. *Management Science, 40*, 429–439.

Wallas, G. (1926). *The art of thought.* New York: Harcourt Brace and World.

Ward, L. (2013, October 11). 10 innovators who changed the world in 2013. *Popular Mechanics.* Retrieved from http://www.popularmechanics.com/technology/g1315/10-innovators-who-changed-the-world-in-2013/?slide=4

Waves for Water. (n.d.). Surf to school: Any kid, anywhere in the world, can host one. Retrieved from http://www.wavesforwater.org/project/surftoschool

Weick, K. (1979). *The social psychology of organizing.* New York: McGraw-Hill.

Weick, K. (1995). *Sensemaking in organizations.* Thousand Oaks, CA: Sage.

Whiteley, G. (Director). (2015). *Most likely to succeed.* One Potato Productions.

Wigfield, A., & Eccles, J. S. (2000). Expectancy–value theory of achievement motivation. *Contemporary Educational Psychology, 25*, 68–81.

Wiliam, D. (2011). *Embedded formative assessment.* Bloomington, IN: Solution Tree.

Woodside, A. G. (2004). Advancing from subjective to confirmatory personal introspection in consumer research. *Psychology & Marketing, 21*, 987–1010.

Yong, E. (2010). Eight-year-old children publish bee study in Royal Society journal [Blog post]. *Discover magazine.* Retrieved from http://blogs.discovermagazine.com/notrocketscience/ 2010/12/21/eight-year-old-children-publish- bee-study-in-royal-society-journal/ #.VM-EckKn14V

Index

Note: Page references followed by an italicized *f* indicate information contained in figures.

About the Author

 **Ronald A. Beghetto** is an internationally recognized expert on creativity in educational settings. He serves as professor of educational psychology in the Neag School of Education and director of the Innovation House at the University of Connecticut. He is editor-in-chief of the *Journal of Creative Behavior* and a fellow of the American Psychological Association and the Society for the Psychology of Aesthetics, Creativity and the Arts (Div. 10, APA).

Dr. Beghetto has published seven books and more than 100 articles and scholarly book chapters on creative and innovative approaches to teaching, learning, and leadership in schools and classrooms. He speaks and provides workshops around the world on issues related to helping teachers and instructional leaders develop new and transformative possibilities for classroom teaching, learning, and leadership in K–12 and higher education settings.

Prior to joining the faculty at UConn, Dr. Beghetto served at the University of Oregon as the College of Education's associate dean for academic affairs and associate professor of education studies. He earned his PhD in educational psychology (with an emphasis in learning, cognition and instruction) from Indiana University. He can be reached at Ron.Beghetto@gmail.com or via his website: www.ronaldbeghetto.com.

Related ASCD Resources

At the time of publication, the following resources were available (ASCD stock numbers appear in parentheses).

Print Products

Authentic Learning in the Digital Age: Engaging Students Through Inquiry by Larissa Pahomov (#115009)

Setting the Standard for Project Based Learning: A Proven Approach to Rigorous Classroom Instruction by John Larmer, John Mergendoller, and Suzie Boss (#114017)

Sparking Student Creativity: Practical Ways to Promote Innovative Thinking and Problem Solving by Patti Drapeau (#115007)

Students at the Center: Personalized Learning with Habits of Mind by Bena Kallick and Allison Zmuda (#117015)

Teaching in the Fast Lane: How to Create Active Learning Experiences by Suzy Pepper Rollins (#117024)

For up-to-date information about ASCD resources, go to **www.ascd.org.** You can search the complete archives of *Educational Leadership* at **www.ascd.org/el**.

Videos

21st Century Skills: Promoting Creativity and Innovation in the Classroom DVD (#609096)

The Innovators: Project Based Learning and the 21st Century DVD (#613043)

ASCD myTeachSource®

Download resources from a professional learning platform with hundreds of research-based best practices and tools for your classroom at http://myteachsource. ascd.org/.

For more information, send an e-mail to member@ascd.org; call 1-800-933-2723 or 703-578-9600; send a fax to 703-575-5400; or write to Information Services, ASCD, 1703 N. Beauregard St., Alexandria, VA 22311-1714 USA.